BACKGAMMON
THE
CRUELEST GAME

Barclay Cooke & Jon Bradshaw

BACKGAMMON THE CRUELEST GAME

RANDOM HOUSE
New York

To Madora

Cooke, Barclay.
Backgammon: The Cruelest Game.
1. Backgammon. I. Bradshaw, Jon, joint author.
II. Title.
GV1469.B2C66   795'.1   74-8725
ISBN 0-394-48812-1

Manufactured in the United States of America

Design by Bernard Klein

98765432

First Edition

CONTENTS

BACKGAMMON
THE
CRUELEST GAME

THE RULES OF THE GAME

Everything is very simple in war, but the
simplest thing is difficult.
                    —*Karl von Clausewitz*

Though backgammon is
one of the most deceptive and difficult of board games and
the most cunning game of chance, its rules are few and
simple and its objectives are easily understood.

The game is normally played by two opponents (though
more than two may play in what is known as *chouette*) on a
board divided into four sections or quadrants. Each quad-
rant is marked with six alternately colored triangles called
points. (See Diagram 1.) Each point has its designated number ranging from 1 to 12 on either side of the board, totaling 24 points in all. These points are referred to by their
numbers, as, for example, the 1 point or the 6 point. Only
the 7 point actually has a name and is called the *bar point*,
since it is next to the bar that divides the board in two. The
colors of the points have no significance other than to dis-
tinguish one from the other.

Each opponent has fifteen men, or checkers; for the
purposes of this book, one opponent's men will be red, the
other white. It might be simpler and would certainly be
accurate to imagine these men as two opposing armies.

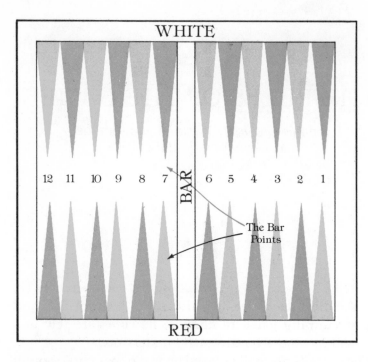

Diagram

1

When the game begins, the two armies are arranged on either side of the board in battle-line formations. (See Diagram 2.) As is apparent, one side is the mirror image of the other. Since, theoretically, it does not matter in which direction you move your men, the board might be set up in exactly the opposite way. (See Diagram 3.) There is no difference between the opening arrangements, but custom dictates that both of the players' inner boards be nearer the source of light. It is an old custom, almost certainly derived from the fact that backgammon, like many other gambling games, tended to be nocturnal and was often played in ill-lit rooms.

Dependent on the rolls of the dice, the object of the game is, as illustrated in Diagram 2, for white to move his men forward in a clockwise direction around and off the

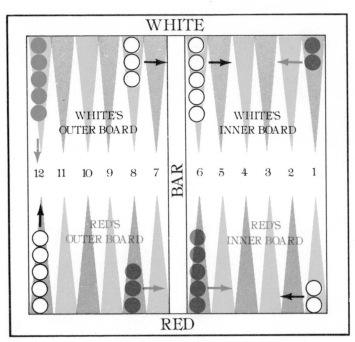

iagram
2

board before red, moving in a counterclockwise direction, can do the same. The men are not permitted to move backwards. Before either player may take any men off, all fifteen of his men must be in his inner board. Taking men off the board is called *bearing off*.

If white, for example, can accomplish this (that is, move his army around and off the board) before red, white wins the game. If white can do this before red has moved all of his men into his own inner board, and has borne at least one man off, white wins a double game or what is called a *gammon*. And, should white accomplish this with any of red's men remaining in white's inner board, white will win a triple game or a *backgammon*. The triple game, incidentally, is an American amendment and is not recognized in England or on the Continent.

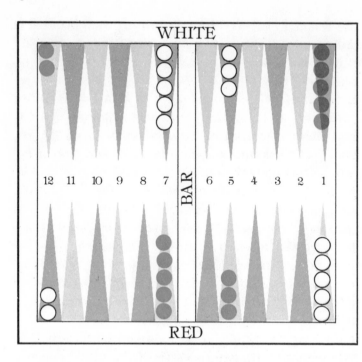

WHITE

| 12 | 11 | 10 | 9 | 8 | 7 | BAR | 6 | 5 | 4 | 3 | 2 | 1 |

RED

Diagram **3**

The men are moved in strict accordance with the rolls of the dice. At the start of every game, each player rolls one die, and the player who has rolled the higher number has the opportunity of playing first—using both resulting numbers. Each player must roll his die into the board at his right. If the dice do not come to rest flat on the board—that is, if either die is angled up against the side of the board or against one of the checkers—it is called *cocked* and must be rolled again. If both players roll the same number, they must re-roll until different numbers appear. Following the opening roll, the players take alternate turns, and each rolls both his dice together.

Let us assume that player A has rolled a 6 and player B a 2. Because player A has rolled the higher number, he is entitled to play first. He has two separate ways in which

o play the 6 and 2; he can move one of his men forward 6
points and another up 2 points, or, using the sum total of
he dice, he can move one man 8 points. Either number
may be played first. In other words, a roll of 6 and 2 may be
played in either of two ways—as a 6-2 or as a 2-6. If, however, a situation arises where only one number can be
moved and there is a choice, it is mandatory to play the
higher one. Let's assume white rolls a 6-2 and that if he
plays the 6, he has no way to move the 2 and vice versa. He
must play the 6 in this instance and forgo the 2. If either
player rolls a double—for example, double 4's—he is
obliged to move that number four times if possible. That
is, he can move one man 16 points or two men 8 points or
two men 4 points and another two men 4 points. This
principle applies to all doubles. In their simplest variations,
these are the basic mechanics employed in the movement of
all the pieces.

The men are permitted to land on any point which is
not already occupied by two or more of the other player's
men. Such *blocks*, as they are called, by two or more of the
other player's men, make or establish the point; they resemble fortified positions, which, so long as there are at
least two enemy men on any one point, remain impregnable. Thus, if player A rolled a 6 and player B had formed a
block 6 points away, player A would not be permitted to
land on that position. If, however, he rolled a 6 and a 3, for
example, he could, provided there were no other enemy
blocks further along, leap across the block by using the 3
first and then the 6. This point is illustrated in Diagram 4.
Here, white has rolled a 6-3 and wishes to move one of
his men on the 1 point forward. Had he rolled two 6's, he
would not have been able to get beyond red's fortified position. But, by employing the 3 first, he is able to hurdle it.

Blocks are crucial to the playing of backgammon. The
more consecutive blocks a player can build, the greater

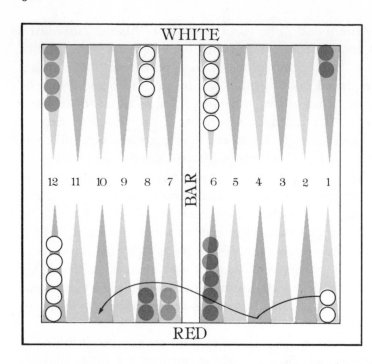

chance he has of imprisoning any of his opponent's men
behind them. They are the military equivalent of a series
of tightly formed barricades. A six-point block—that is,
two men positioned on each of six consecutive points—
constitutes what is called a *prime*. Because the largest
number a player can roll is a 6, a prime prevents the enemy
from hurdling over it. An example of a prime is shown in
Diagram 5. Obviously, any lesser number of consecutive
blocks, such as a four- or a five-point block, is not as
strong as a prime, but is very valuable in restricting the
movement of enemy men.

Men which are not a part of a block—that is, those
men occupying points by themselves—are called *blots*. In
military terms, such men resemble stragglers, who are either lost or have become separated from the main body of

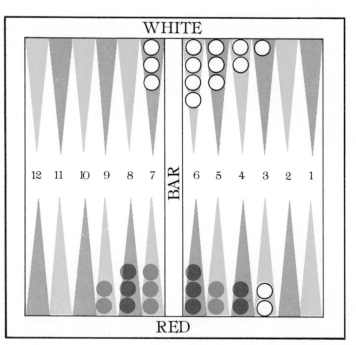

agram
5

their army, and as a result are relatively easy targets of attack. In Diagram 6, for example, the enemy, providing he rolls the exact number (in this instance, a 3-6 or 4-5), can land on red's open man, or blot. This form of capture is called *hitting a blot*. Any open and unprotected man is a potential prisoner. (Often, however, it is not as foolhardy as it may appear to leave blots intentionally in order to increase your options of movement, but this is a more subtle tactical maneuver, which we will discuss in subsequent chapters.)

Since a player must complete his full roll—that is, play both numbers—and since it is not always possible to land safely on your own secure positions, both are often forced to leave blots up and down the board. If one of your blots is captured by your opponent, regardless of how far

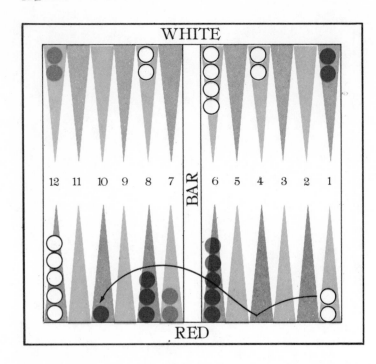

WHITE

12 11 10 9 8 7 BAR 6 5 4 3 2 1

RED

Diagr
6

your man has advanced, he is sent back to the beginning (or, as it is called, *put on the bar*). The captured man is literally placed upon the bar that divides the board and must remain there until he is able to enter the game again. Given the continual struggle being waged up and down the board, it is possible for both players to have captured men on the bar at the same time, and for one player, or both, to have several men on the bar.

Captured men are permitted to re-enter the game only when they have rolled a number that corresponds to the number of a point in their opponent's inner board which is not occupied by two or more of the opponent's men. For example, in Diagram 7, one of white's men has been captured and has been placed on the bar. Since red has established blocks on his 6 and 5 points, white, should he

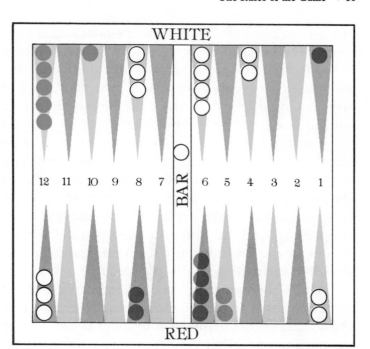

iagram
7

roll either a 6 or a 5, would not be able to come in on either of those two points. Specifically, if he rolled a 6-5, double 5's or double 6's, he could not come in at all. A roll of 6-2, however, would mean that he could come in on the 2 point, but not on the 6 point, and would have to play his 6 elsewhere. Obviously, then, the more blocks a player can erect in his inner board (assuming that at least one of the enemy men has been captured), the less chance his opponent will have of re-entering the game.

In the ideal defensive position, red blocks all the points in his inner board, establishing what is called a *closed board*. Should white have a captured man on the bar, he will not be able to re-enter the game at all—at least until red decides or is forced into opening one of his points. This is one of the game's main strategies—to capture one or more of your opponent's men and to close your board completely, thereby shutting off all means of escape. For as long as either player has a man on the bar, he is not permitted to move elsewhere until that man is returned to play. A closed board, then, is the perfect defensive position, equivalent to a naval blockade.

The final method of moving your men is when you actually bear them off the board. When the game begins, it is already one-third over in one sense, since five of your fifteen men are already in your inner board. The object of the game, as previously explained, is to move all the rest of your men around and into your inner board. Only when all are in can you begin bearing them off, and the player who gets all of them off first wins the game.

Again, the men are borne off in accordance with the numbers shown on the rolled dice. As in the three other sections, there are six points in your inner board. Assume that you have moved all of your men into your inner board as shown in Diagram 8. If white now rolls a 4-2, he is permitted to take one man off his 4 point and another off his 2 point. If he rolls double 4's, he is permitted to take three men off his 4 point and can then move his remaining 4 down four points from the 6 point or down four points from his 5 point. Because there was not a fourth 4 on his 4 point, he is not able to bear another man off. This would also hold true had he rolled a 1. As there are no men on his 1 point, he will have to move a 1 elsewhere in his inner board. You must use your entire roll. For example, if white did not have any men on his 6 point and rolled a 6, he would take one man off his next lowest point on which there were men. This rule is implemented on a descending scale, so that if, for example, white has only two men left on his 1 point and he rolls a 6-5, he can take them both off. The same rule applies to doubles. To repeat: the

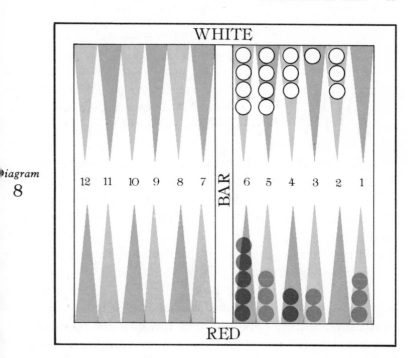

Diagram
8

player who bears off all of his men first wins the game.

These, then, are the simple, almost nursery-game rules of backgammon. Of course the game's apparent simplicity is its initial attraction. But its simplicity is of infinite variety, and is an amalgam of science and art. As with any dice game, luck plays its customary role. Skill is employed first by learning the rules and then by knowing the percentages and probabilities—when to play offense or defense, when to block and when to run. But it is important to understand these fundamentals before going on to more arcane and complicated matters. There is much more to backgammon than what the Penguin *Dictionary of English* innocently defines as "a hinged board with draughtsmen and dice," but it is well to begin with that.

BASIC OPENING MOVES AND A FEW ESSENTIAL REPLIES

Whatever is to the advantage of one side
is to the disadvantage of the other.[*]
—*Karl von Clausewitz*

As explained in the previous chapter, once each player has cast his opening die, the player who has rolled the higher number begins the game, using both his and his opponent's numbers. Thus, if player A has rolled a 2 and player B a 6, player B must now play a 6 and a 2. These are the game's opening shots, the initial sally into the battlefield, and they should not be played at random.

As in any conflict, at the outset there are certain sound strategic moves to be made, and since these moves will almost certainly influence the enemy's subsequent actions, they must be utilized to your best advantage. Immediately, therefore, a campaign strategy must be devised, the sole purpose of which is the ultimate surrender or destruction of the enemy forces.

The opening moves are the first step in this direction and, unlike other parts of the game, they should almost always be played in certain tactical ways. These moves can and should be learned by rote. They are simple but important ploys, the aim of which is to seek or establish strong opening positions.

Depending on the dice, of course, there are both favorable and unfavorable opening rolls, and the odds, alas, are 25 to 11 (coincidentally, the most familiar fraction in backgammon, which you will get to know well in Chapter Four) against obtaining a favorable opening roll. The good opening rolls are any double (except double 5's), 3-1, 4-2 and 6-1. (Theoretically, only the second player can open with a double.) These rolls establish strong positions or beachheads from which it is possible to launch subsequent assaults. All other rolls, in varying degree, are unfavorable. In our view, 6-5 is an unfavorable opening roll, since it leaves the back man unprotected and contributes nothing to the strengthening of your position. In fact, *any* 5 on the opening roll is weak and inauspicious.

In order of preference the opening rolls are

1-1	6-2
6-6	6-4
3-3, 4-4, 2-2	6-3
3-1	5-5
4-2, 6-1	2-1, 4-1
6-5	5-1
3-2	5-4
4-3	5-2
5-3	

To repeat: the opening moves should almost always be played in the same way. We say "almost," since, if you are rolling second, you may have to alter certain moves in order to combat the opening roll of your opponent. (These tactics will be discussed later in the chapter.)

Assuming you are playing first, the opening rolls should be played in the manner suggested below. (Go back and consult the opening position shown in Diagram 2 and assume that you are red.)

1-1 — Bring two men from red's 8 point to red's 7, or bar point, and two men from red's 6 point to red's 5 point. This invaluable roll establishes an immediate three-point block incorporating two important points — red's bar point and 5 point. There is no better way of playing this best of all opening rolls. (See Diagram 9.)

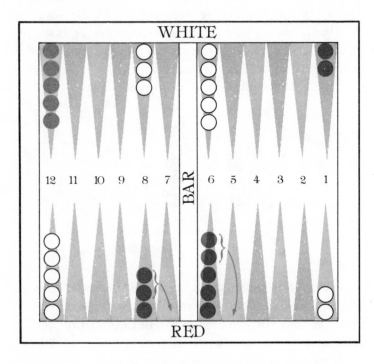

Diagram 9

6-6—Bring two men from white's 1 point to white's bar point and two men from white's 12 point to red's bar point. You have now established superb offensive and defensive positions and are off to a commanding lead. (See Diagram 10.)

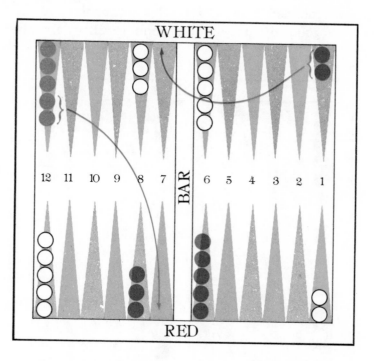

Diagram
10

3-3—Bring two men from red's 8 point to red's 5 point and two men from white's 1 point to white's 4 point. With this roll there are alternative plays. Some favor moving two men from white's 12 point to red's bar point, but this play may best be described as atrocious. Though it does block sixes rolled by your opponent, your own bar point is not that important

this early in the game. More importantly, there are
better plays. Another alternative is to bring two men
from red's 8 point to red's 5 point and two men from
red's 6 point down to red's 3 point—thereby giving
red three immediate points in his inner board. It is a
good offensive play, but second-best. Our recommended play achieves two immediate advantages: a
good offense and a good defense. Its alternative

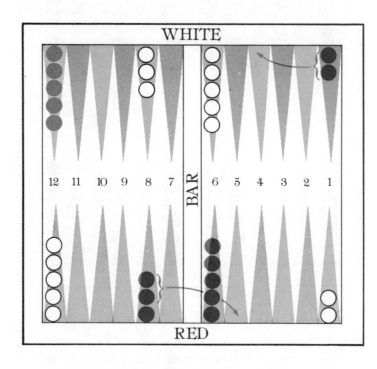

Diagram
11

(making the two points in red's inner board) might
be effectively employed in a tournament, for example, should red require a double game, * but in most

*This will be discussed in Chapter Seven.

cases your position is not considerably improved by making the extra point, particularly in view of the other, better defensive play of bringing two men up from white's 1 point. An additional advantage of this play is that it renders white's 5 point, should he make it early in the game, much less valuable than it would normally be. (See Diagram 11.)

4-4 — Bring two men from white's 1 point up to white's 5 point and two men from red's 8 point down to red's 4 point. It is true that the blot on red's 8 point now becomes vulnerable to any roll of white's totaling 7, but it also negates his ordinarily good roll of 6-1,

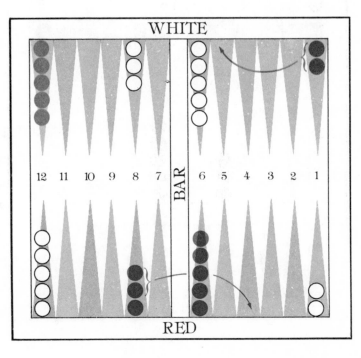

iagram
12

since he will probably use it to hit red rather than making his own bar point. Our recommended play employs the best offensive and defensive tactics. Instead of the 4 point, most experts recommend making red's 9 point, but we prefer the former play. (See Diagram 12.)

2-2 — Our recommended play is to bring two men from white's 12 point to red's 11 point and two men from red's 6 point to red's 4 point. This is a strong attacking position. Alternatively, should you have less experience than your opponent, you might bring

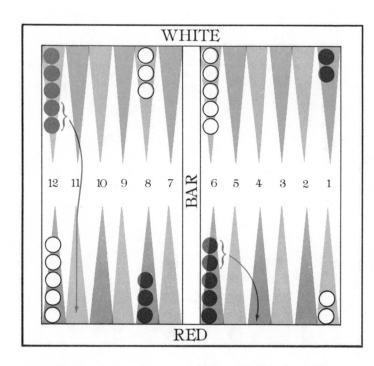

Diagram

13

two men up from white's 1 point to white's 5 point. It is seldom wrong to make your opponent's 5 point, and it is an excellent defensive position. Double 2's probably have more "correct" variations than any other double on the opening roll. (See Diagram 13.)

3-1 — This is the golden shot to make the golden point. Move one man from red's 8 point to red's 5 point and one man from red's 6 point to red's 5 point. Excluding doubles, there is no more advantageous opening roll. (See Diagram 14.)

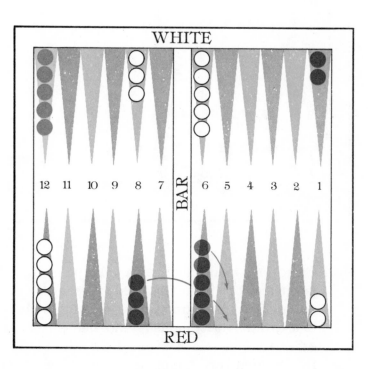

Diagram 14

4-2 — Bring one man from red's 8 point to red's 4 point
and another man from red's 6 point to red's 4 point,
thereby establishing red's 4 point. Since this roll
establishes a valuable point in red's inner board, it
is every bit as good a roll as 6-1, although probably
not considered so by many players. (See Diagram 15.)

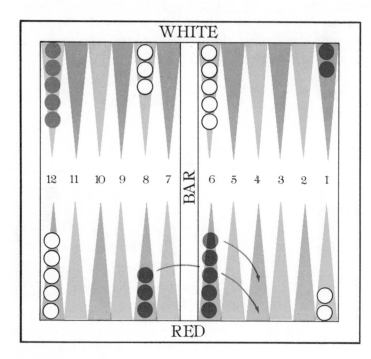

WHITE

12 11 10 9 8 7 BAR 6 5 4 3 2 1

RED

Diagram
15

6-1 — Bring one man from white's 12 point to red's bar
point and one man from red's 8 point to red's bar
point. This is a strong play, creating a three-point
block, but it accomplishes no immediate objective
other than to block sixes. However, there are no
real alternatives, though some experts when seeking

involvement against weaker players have been known to move one man from white's 12 point to their bar point and another man from their 6 point to their 5 point, thereby leaving two directly assaultable blots. It is a droll but insupportable play and is not to be recommended. (See Diagram 16.)

agram
16

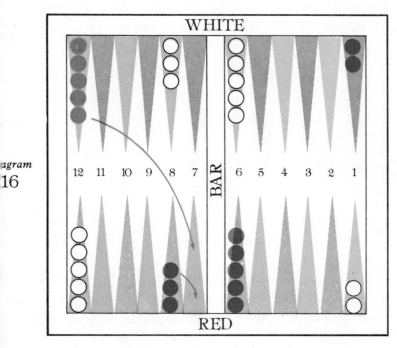

6-5 — Bring one man from white's 1 point all the way out to white's 12 point. In backgammon parlance, this move is referred to as the *lover's leap*. There is no good alternative. The 6-5 separates the favorable from the unfavorable rolls. It is not particularly advantageous and it forces red into an early running game. (See Diagram 17.)

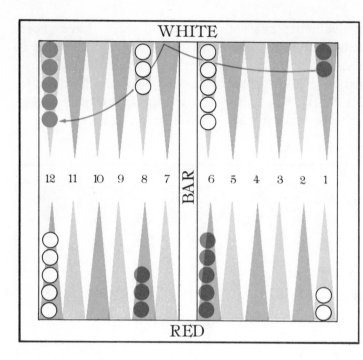

3-2 — Bring two men down from white's 12 point, placing
one of them on red's 11 point and the other on red's
10 point. Since red is vulnerable only to a roll of
or 10 by white, he is relatively secure and in an ex
cellent position to create additional points. There i
an alternative — bringing one man from white's 1
point to red's 11 point and dropping one man from
red's 8 point to red's 5 point. If red is not hit, he i
in a good position to make his 5 point on his nex
roll. But a roll of 4 will hit and double 4's could b
a serious blow. The first play is superior. (See Dia
gram 18.)

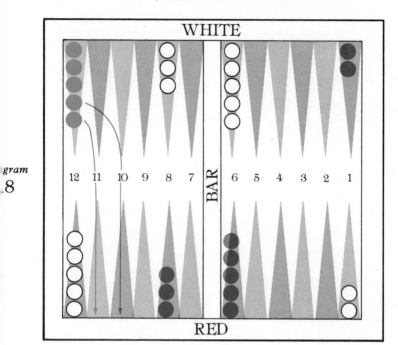

4-3—Bring two men from white's 12 point to red's 9 and
10 points. Again, this gives red the potential to create new points. Although vulnerable to rolls totaling
8 or 9, this is still the most effective play. There are
no happier alternatives. (See Diagram 19.)

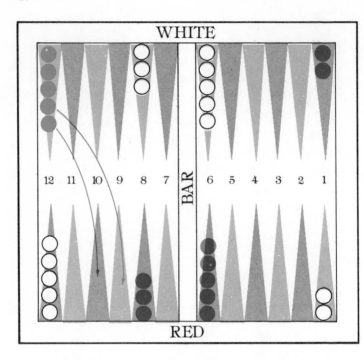

WHITE

12 11 10 9 8 7 | BAR | 6 5 4 3 2 1

RED

Diagr
1

5-3 — Bring down two men from white's 12 point, placing them on red's 8 and 10 points. It is true that your blot is vulnerable to a roll of 9, but should it not be hit, this play, on red's next move, changes lackluster rolls of 5-1, 4-1, 6-3, 6-2 or another 5-3 into good rolls. It also improves subsequent rolls of 4-3, 3-2 and 2-1. Some experts have suggested establishing red's 3 point with a roll of 5-3, but it is an inferior play. At this point in the game, the 3 point is almost irrelevant; it does not become really valuable until the 5 and 4 points have been secured. (See Diagram 20.)

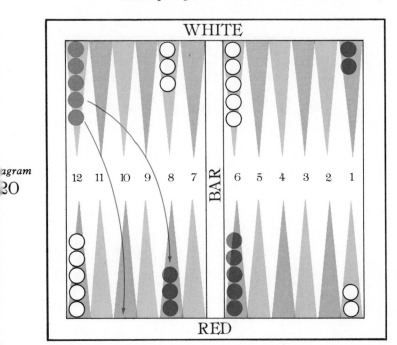

6-2 — Bring one man from white's 12 point all the way to red's 5 point. To bring one man from white's 1 point out to white's 9 point is not as good a play. Both plays can be hit by a 4, though double 1's cannot hit the 6-2 brought out to white's 9 point. Although double 1's can hit the exposed man on red's 5 point, a good player would never make this play, so the odds in both instances are even. At this early stage in the game, it is well worth gambling to secure red's 5 point. Red is exposed only to a roll of 4 or a combination totaling 4. Any other alternatives are even less satisfactory. (See Diagram 21.)

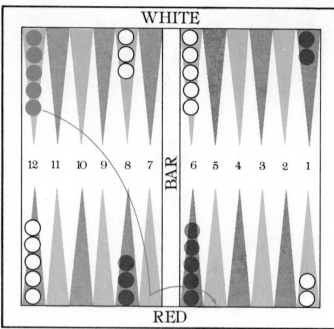

WHITE

12 11 10 9 8 7 BAR 6 5 4 3 2 1

RED

Diagr
21

6-4 — Bring one man from white's 1 point to white's 11
point. In this play red is exposed to a direct 2, but i
not hit, he has released one man and placed him in a
position to create new points in his outer board. It i:
not recommended that red make his 2 point with thi:
roll. Such a play accomplishes nothing except to ad
vance two men too far too early. (See Diagram 22.)

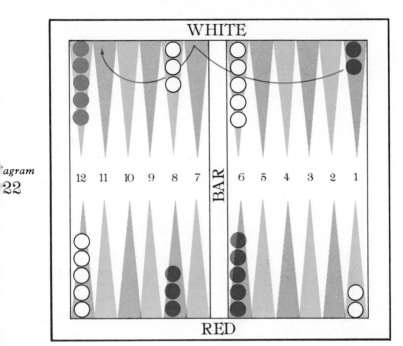

6-3 — Bring one man from white's 1 point out to white's 10 point. There is no satisfactory alternative. Red is now vulnerable to a direct 3. This is a shade worse than 6-4, since it is 25 to 11 that a 2 will not be hit but 23 to 13 that the exposed 3 will not be hit. Nonetheless, it is the best way to play this altogether unsatisfactory roll. (See Diagram 23.)

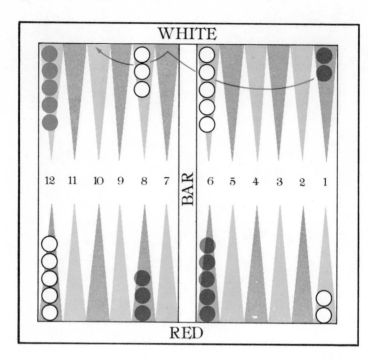

Diagra
23

5-5 — Bring two men from white's 12 point all the way to red's 3 point. This roll is the most odious of doubles. It accomplishes relatively little and forces two men more or less out of position. It becomes especially awkward when followed by further 5's. (See Diagram 24.)

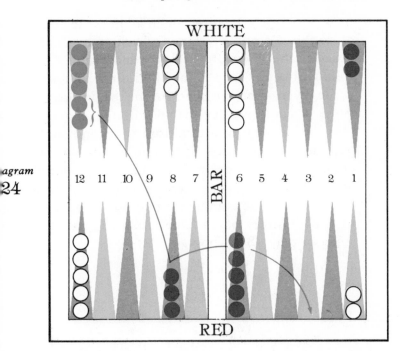

agram
24

2-1 — Bring one man from white's 12 point to red's 11
point and another man from red's 6 point to red's
5 point. This is an unfortunate roll, but red has no
better option than to attempt to secure his 5 point.
He is exposed to a direct 4, but if he is not hit, his
chances of establishing his 5 point are much improved. Under no circumstances should red split his
back men by moving a man from white's 1 point to
white's 2 point. At this stage in the game, white's 1
point is red's main security. Were red to separate
those two men, he would become vulnerable to double 5's, and a 4-1. Dropping an exposed man on
red's 5 point is considered bold by the inexperienced
player. In fact, it is less bold than separating the two

men on white's 1 point, for in addition to the threat
of double 5's and a 4-1, red's back men are also exposed to the threat of double 4's and double 6's. Such
rolls will occur only 5 out of 36 times, but why give
white even that chance? In the beginning of the
game, it could well be the end. In our recommended
play, red is open to attack from any 4 and could lose
both men should his opponent roll a 6-4—white's
perfect shot. But even if red then rolled double 6's
and was unable to re-enter, he would still be in the
game because he commands that one defensive point
in white's inner board. Our initial suggestion is the
superior play. (See Diagram 25.)

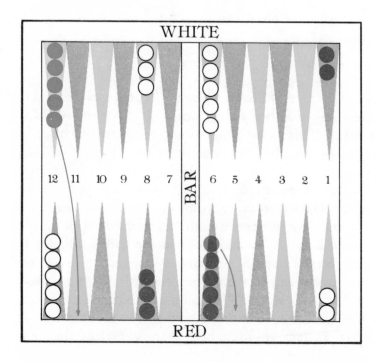

Diagram
25

4-1 — Bring one man from white's 12 point to red's 9 point and drop another man from red's 6 point to red's 5 point. This is a good offensive move. Again red is exposed to a 4, and double 4's would capture both men, but it is still the best play. The problem with both the 4-1 and the 2-1 is that nothing constructive is immediately accomplished. Red is only preparing to make points and is therefore vulnerable. Even so, should the blots not be hit, red's position is potentially strong. (See Diagram 26.)

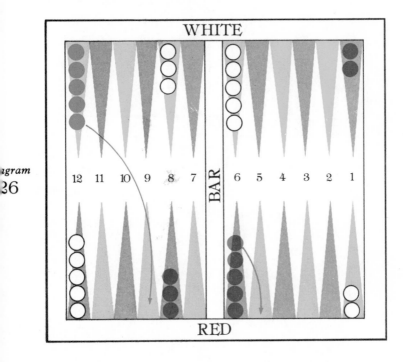

Diagram 26

5-1 — Bring one man from white's 12 point to red's 8 point and drop another man from red's 6 point to red's 5

point. All opening 5's are clumsy; any other roll has
greater promise. An alternative play would be to bring
a man from white's 12 point to red's bar point, but
this is not as valuable a point to attempt to secure
at this early stage of the game. Although unsafe, it
is best to gamble in order to secure the important
5 point. Again, red should not split the two men on
white's 1 point; the risks are serious and the rewards
slight. (See Diagram 27.)

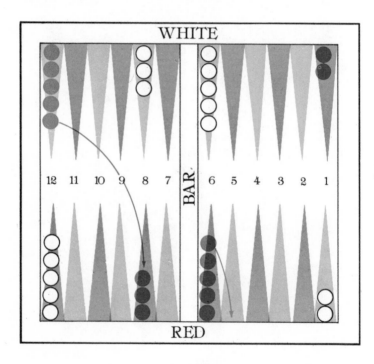

Diagram
27

5-4—Bring two men from white's 12 point to red's 9 and
8 points. Red is exposed to any 8, but it is a better

lay than bringing one man from white's 1 point out
o white's 10 point, where red would be vulnerable
o a direct 3. Red has acquired nine *pips* (or points)
nd should not relinquish them lightly. The one
lrawback to our recommended play is that red adds
n irrelevant man to his 8 point, but the play is pre-
erred for the extra builder he acquires on his 9
oint. (See Diagram 28.)

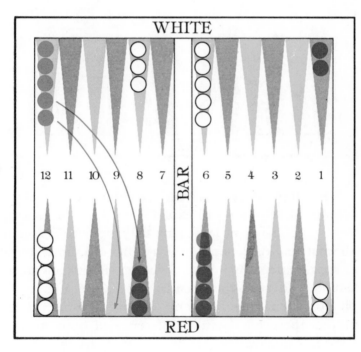

igram
28

-2 — Bring two men from white's 12 point to red's 11 and
     8 points. This is the worst of opening rolls. There
     are no good alternative plays. (See Diagram 29.)

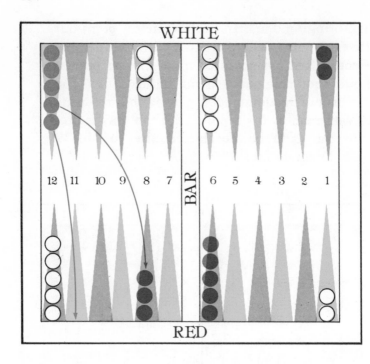

Diagr
29

At this stage, having recommended certain basic opening moves, we will explain just why we believe them to be correct—or at least why they are sounder than their alternatives. Backgammon is a game of infinite variations, of specific departures and deviations from general rules of thumb, and even the opening moves are affected by this phenomenon. For as long as backgammon has been played, there has been a difference of opinion as to the "correct" deployment of the various opening rolls. To this day, only 8 of the 21 opening rolls are generally agreed upon—1-1, 5-5, 6-6, 3-1, 4-2, 6-1, 6-5 and 5-2. The other 13 all seem to have acceptable alternatives and are played differently by different players. In each case where no certainty has existed, it has been our aim to give what we believe to be the best tactical alternative.

For instance, for years it was thought correct with opening rolls of 5-1, 4-1 and 2-1 to use the 1 to split the two men in the opponent's inner board; few players deployed the 1 in any other way. Gradually, however, the alternative of using the 1 to start your own 5 point was employed, and both moves began to seem equally advantageous. After continual study and analysis, we are now firmly convinced that a player should not split those back men immediately. The paradox of the "gambling" play of starting your 5 point, as opposed to the "conservative" play of splitting the back men, is intriguing, for in reality, the split is infinitely more of a gamble than its alternative.

But since we are so against the splitting of the back men, why do we recommend coming out all the way with opening rolls of 6-3 and 6-4? The remaining back man is vulnerable to double 5's, and it is quite possible that both blots will be hit. Again, the reason for moving the 6-3 and 6-4 in this way is that there is really no better alternative. To start your bar with the 6 and to bring another man to the 9 point with the 4 (or to the 10 point with the 3) is a possible alternative, but it is not recommended because we feel it is too much to ask the novice to begin the game in such apparently prodigal fashion. However, once you have learned to play and have acquired some confidence, there is no reason why you should not bring two men down to your bar and your 9 or 10 point with an opening 6-3 or 6-4. This is especially sound when you are the more skillful player, since you are seeking the kind of involvement in which your superior technical skills will weigh most heavily. Conversely, when competing against better players, try to seek simple positions.

The double 4's opening seems so logical that we cannot account for its not having been recommended elsewhere. You will have noticed that we suggest you play

opening double 4's and double 3's in much the sam
way—that is, by establishing one point in your own board
and a forward point in your opponent's board. Most expert
like making their 9 point and the enemy 5 point with
double 4's and two points in their inner board with double
3's. There is nothing *wrong* with these plays, but by play
ing double 4's and double 3's as we recommend, you have
achieved an equilibrium of forces—a balanced position
from which it is possible both to attack and to defend—and
therefore it seems to us that in total assets, you are dis
tinctly ahead.

An intriguing phenomenon is at work here. When you
begin to play backgammon, you are shown the opening
positions, the movements of the men are explained, and
you are told that the game's object is a race between two
opposing armies. Thus, when you have opening rolls of
5-1, 4-1, 2-1, 4-3 or 3-2, your natural first reaction is to
play as safely as you can, avoid capture, get around the
board, bear off and win. The beginner's instinctive inclina
tion is to think, "Why should I expose a man on my 5
point, which, if hit, will have to go all the way back to the
beginning again, whereas if I expose a man in my oppo
nent's inner board by splitting the two back men, it will
not cost me nearly so much if hit?"

This argument is spurious, because when such rolls
as these ten (5-1, 4-1, 2-1, 4-3, 3-2) occur on the opening
roll, the game's running element is temporarily suspended
in favor of attempting to establish offensive and defensive
positions. Should you employ a 1 on the opening roll to
start your 5 point and it is hit, no disaster has occurred
but it *might* prove to be disastrous if you split your back
men and one or both of them are hit.

There are even certain minor advantages to being hit
on your 5 point, since a subsequent roll of 5-4, ordinarily

liability, allows you to make your opponent's 5 point, nd subsequent rolls of 4-3, 3-2 and even 2-1 allow you to stablish forward positions in your opponent's board. A ubsequent roll of double 6's, of course, would be comletely wasted, but one cannot expect a panacea.

With an opening roll of 2-1, a possible alternative to ur recommended play would be to move one man from our opponent's 12 point to your own 10 point. The movenent of the 2-1 is somewhat different from the 5-1 and -1, since you can play the 1 in your outer board. With he 5-1 and the 4-1, you are almost forced to start your 5 oint, since it is inadvisable to use the 1 in your outer board y dropping it on your bar point, or, in the case of 4-1, to tack more men on your 8 point. To start the bar point is vrong because it is not as valuable as the 5 point; besides, he man exposed on the bar point is more likely to be hit han the exposed man on the 5 point.

In the early stages of the game, the difference in value etween the 5 point and the bar point cannot be overemhasized. The most important reason for this is that if you ave made the 5 point and your opponent is hit and then olls any 5, he is necessarily restricted. He must enter with he other number and then play the 5 elsewhere in his oard. Had you made the bar point instead, this restriction vould not exist. The bar point does block double 6's, but he 5 point blocks double 4's. The advantage of the 5 point ver the bar point remains clear-cut. Conversely, if you ccupy your opponent's 5 point, he will think twice about ringing blots into his outer board, since they will be in he direct line of your fire.

Backgammon, in fact, is centered around the 5 points. They are the fulcrums around which the game revolves. When your opponent secures one, you must attempt to ecure the other. This is the chief reason for dropping a 1

to the 5 point on opening rolls of 5-1, 4-1 and 2-1. Give
the great value of the point, it is worth almost any risk t
secure it.

These, then, are our suggested opening moves, and w
have attempted to present reasonable arguments in favor o
each of them. They are fundamental to the playing of th
game—first principles, tactical probes of the enemy's pos
tion. The object of any opening campaign strategy is t
reach a position by disciplined maneuvering in which on
army has acquired a tactical advantage over the othe
These are the first sure steps in that direction. As soon a
you have learned these opening moves, you will know onl
a small fraction of what you have to know in order to pla
backgammon well. But it is a start, and an important on
Learn these moves by heart.

Essential Replies to Basic Opening Moves

Following the opening move, backgammon is n
longer a game of routine—and having been learned, man
basic principles must be temporarily put aside. This be
comes immediately apparent when both players have con
pleted their opening moves, and this will be discussed i
detail in Chapter Three. When just one player has con
pleted his opening roll, however, and the other player ha
not yet moved, some of our suggested opening maneuver
have to be altered in order to combat the new position th
first player has created in the board.

For example, in Diagram 30, white has played a
opening 6-1, and red now rolls double 6's. It would no
as some experts suggest, be advisable to move four me
down from white's 12 point to red's bar point. The recon
mended play is to move two men down from white's 1

point to red's bar point, and two men from red's 8 point to red's 2 point. This play prevents red from breaking white's 12 point early in the game — an unusually bad practice.

In Diagram 31, white has again played an opening roll of 6-1 and red now rolls a 6-5. Since white's bar point is blocked, red cannot run one man from white's 1 point out to white's 12 point as he would normally do. It is best, therefore, to move two men down from white's 12 point to red's 8 and bar points. Do not move one man from white's 12 point down to red's 2 point. It accomplishes nothing, and since red must gamble in this situation, it would be best for him to place a blot on his bar point, since it is more valuable to secure if not hit.

When white has opened with a roll of 6-1, most of

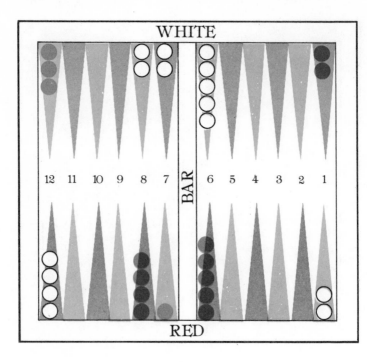

WHITE

12 11 10 9 8 7 BAR 6 5 4 3 2 1

RED

Diagr.
31

red's other standard opening replies should be played as suggested earlier. There are those experts who recommend moving the 5-4, the 4-3 and the 3-2 differently—that is by bringing up one man from white's 1 point before they are hemmed in—but this is a flagrant error. If red ever contemplated such a move, it would be better if he did it *before* white had made his bar point. But either way, it is wrong. His point in white's inner board has now become red's chief defensive block, and it is incorrect to abandon it here. These tactics in no way are cowardly. They are simply common sense, attempting to use what assets red has to best advantage. Never be craven, but don't be foolhardy either.

In Diagram 32, white has completed an opening roll

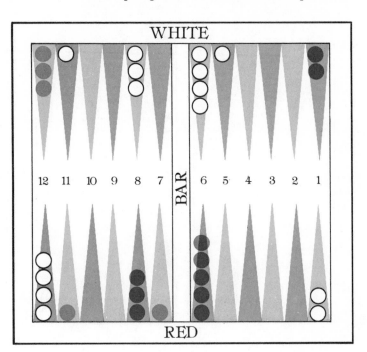

of 2-1 and red responds with a 6-2. In normal circumstances, we have suggested that red move one man from
white's 12 point to his own 5 point. But the circumstances
have now changed. In this instance, red's best answer to
the 2-1 is to bring two men down from white's 12 point,
placing them on his own 11 and bar points. It is a sound
offensive play. Red is vulnerable to a direct 6, but white
may want to use a 6 to cover his blot on the 5 point. Any 6,
3 or 1 covers this blot, so it would be unwise for red to
expose a man to being hit by a 4. *Whenever possible, if you
have to leave a blot, try to have it vulnerable to being hit
by a number that your opponent could use elsewhere to his
advantage.*

In Diagram 33, if white has had an opening roll of 4-

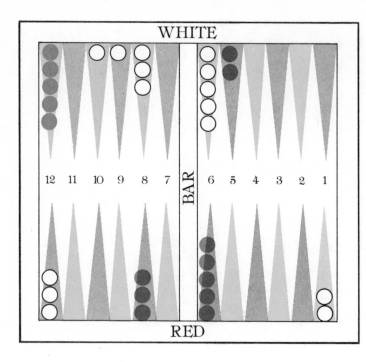

WHITE

12 11 10 9 8 7 | BAR | 6 5 4 3 2 1

Diagr

33

RED

3, red's correct response, should he now roll double 2's, is
to bring two men up from white's 1 point to white's 5
point. This is a valuable defensive play and nullifies the
threat of white's outer builders. If white had opened with
3-2, 5-2 or 5-4, red would play the double 2's this same
way. Under no circumstances should red use the 2's to hit
a man in the outer board.

In Diagram 34, white has rolled an opening 6-3, and
instead of making our recommended play, has started red's
bar point with one man and has moved the other man from
red's 12 point to his own 10 point. Red now rolls double
6's. In this instance, it would not be a weak play for red to
hit white twice, making his own 1 point. Admittedly, this
contradicts not only our suggested opening play for double

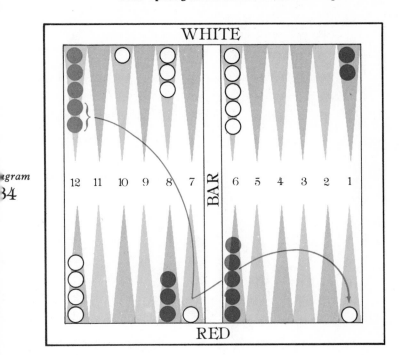

's, but also the general rule of never establishing the 1 point early in the game. Nonetheless, red now has two points in his inner board and two of white's men on the bar. Should white now roll a 6 or a 1 — and he is a 5 to 4 favorite to do so — thereby bringing only one man back into play, red may be able to blitz him before white can get started again. However, if red is the weaker player, it would be more sensible for him to use his double 6's to make both bar points, as originally recommended.

Again, in Diagram 35, if white has had an opening roll of 6-3 and runs a man from red's 1 point out to red's 10 point, and red now responds with a 6-3, red should hit white's blot and start his own bar point. The same principle would apply if red had rolled a 6-4, except that in this

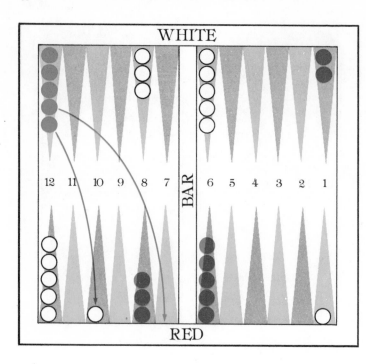

case, red would start white's bar point in order to comba
white's blot. These are dangerous and aggressive counter;
but they are recommended.

In Diagram 36, if white has had an opening roll c
either 5-1, 4-1 or 2-1, and instead of making our recom
mended play, moves the 1 from red's 1 point to red's .
point, and red responds with an opening roll of 4-1, h
should, once again, deviate from the suggested openin;
move. In this case the correct move is to hit white twice b
moving a man from red's 6 point to his 1 point. On thi
specific occasion, 4-1 becomes a reasonably good openin;
move.

In Diagram 37, if red has an opening roll of 3-1 an

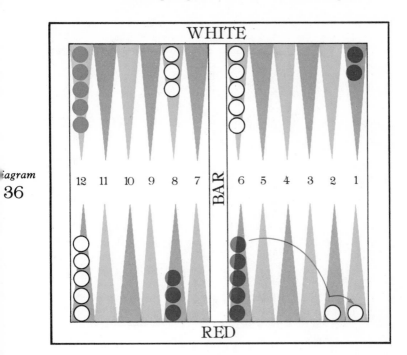

makes his 5 point, and white responds with 3-2, he should adhere to our recommended opening move. This principle would also apply if he had rolled a 4-3. More than ever, white should be wary of splitting his back men. White's best chance to combat red's initial advantage is to bring two builders into his outer board in order to counter-attack. To split inside, thereby weakening his chief defense, is folly, and yet certain experts continue to recom-mend it.

A good general rule: When in doubt, hit. But there must be a doubt! For example, in Diagram 38, white has opened with a 5-1 and has dropped his 1 onto his 5 point. Red now rolls a 3-1. Ordinarily red would make his 5

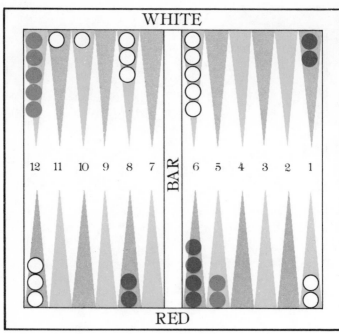

WHITE

12 11 10 9 8 7 BAR 6 5 4 3 2 1

RED

Diagra
37

point, but in this case he should hit white's exposed man. In fact, red should do this with any 4 except for double 1's. There is certainly no doubt as to how double 1's should be played.

As must now be apparent, the astute player learns to change or modify even the most routine of moves, even as early as on the opening roll. Other than these important variations, almost all other responses to opening moves should be played in the suggested way—except, of course, when it is possible to hit an exposed man. The most interesting opening variations occur when the player rolling second throws a double. This will be discussed further in

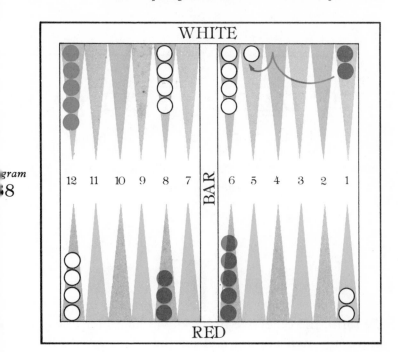

gram
58

Chapter Three because these moves are not only interesting, but illustrate how rapidly the game changes shape and
direction.

◄3►

THE TACTICS OF THE GAME

Military tactics are the integral means
through which the enemy's destruction or
submission is the ultimate end.
— Karl von Clausewitz

Expressed in its most sin
ple form, the objective of backgammon is for one player t
move his men around and off the board before his oppo
nent can do the same. Regardless of what tactics eithe
player employs, this is the game's guiding principle. I
order to do this most effectively, the good player learns t
establish certain defensive and offensive positions. Thu
the object of the game is to run, but its method is to see
secure and unassailable positions, the most important o
which are the two 5 points.

To illustrate this: take the opening rolls of 6-2, 5-
4-1 and 2-1. If the sole strategy of the game were to ru
each of these rolls would be moved as far as they coul
go. But this would be a losing proposition, since it woul
greatly reduce the options of play. However, if these rol
are played correctly, as suggested in Chapter Two, they a
employed primarily to seek position. They are little mo
than minor risks by which the player hopes to acqui
major territorial gains.

From the start, there is a complicated interplay of pos-
bilities, probabilities, good fortune and bad, which in-
uences every facet of the game. In backgammon, to seek
osition is to take certain calculated risks, and because all
layers are ruled by the dictates of the dice — or by chance,
hich Karl von Clausewitz, the nineteenth-century mili-
ry theorist, described as "an agency indifferent to the
ctor's preference for the outcomes" — no player is ever
ntirely in control of his particular destiny. One of the
ame's chief tactics, then, is to shield oneself against the
ice. The player with the stronger position can withstand
greater number of unfavorable rolls, or "bad luck," than
an the more weakly positioned player, who, because he
as failed to protect himself, is more easily assaulted and
verrun.

Nonetheless, no matter how cunningly you play, you
re virtually always vulnerable. One unexpected horror roll
an undermine the best positions and derange the most
ensible of plans; this is both the charm and the frustration
f the game. The best players of backgammon know that
ney must employ the craftiest of tactics, not because of the
ice, but *in spite of* them. It is the enormously high luck
ictor in backgammon that causes it to be a game of skill.
Vithout luck or accident, the game would not only be
onotonous, but infinitely less skillful.

In backgammon, to be skillful is to be self-protective.
t any given point in the game, the better players are aware
f Murphy's Law, which states that "If anything can go
vrong, it will." Given the whimsical nature of the dice,
ll players have a chance in the game, but some players
ave more chances than others because they have created
n environment in which the propitious is more likely to
ccur.

"Running game," then, is a misnomer. Unless both

players throw two consecutive opening 6-5's, the running game in itself is incomprehensible, a contradiction in terms. In backgammon there is no neat and tidy sprint along the flat; the game is more in the nature of a steeple chase and the race is rarely won by the merely swift. The better the player, in fact, the less anxious he is to commit himself to a race. A race is a crap-shoot, and so the better player seeks involvement—conflict with the enemy, in which his superior technical skills will prevail. There must be contact and constant jockeying for position. Developing position is the paramount part of the early game. The first decision as to whether to run or to stay and fight is made on the opening roll and usually will shift and change repeatedly in the course of a single game.

Therefore the accepted notion that backgammon is neatly divided into such concepts as the running game and the blocking game can be dispensed with. To see backgammon in this way is to misunderstand the game's primary strategies. Like chess, backgammon is almost exclusively a game of position. It is no coincidence that chess is played with soldiers and knights, castles and kings. In both theory and practice, chess and backgammon are games of war and depend upon exact and useful strategies.

As has been stated, the basics are relatively simple, but early on you must learn when to make certain moves which are exactly contrary to the basics you have been taught. Some players never grasp this. No sooner does the game start than immediate adjustments must be made because of your opponent's position. For instance, assume that you open with a 6-5 and the enemy counters with 1-1. You now roll 6-1. Hit him instead of making your bar. Here it is only your second roll, and already you are being told to play it in a new manner.

It may help you to overcome these apparent contradic-

ons if you look upon all four segments of the board as a
attlefield. You must try to be as strong as possible in
very area. If you have an impregnable defense—say, a
rong back game—you can become as daring as you wish,
aving blots everywhere. If you have a strong offense—
uch as having the enemy behind a prime—you can safely
eaken your defense. Attempt to establish one or the
ther, and try not to be weak in both at the same time.

Imagine a general, a Bonaparte, astride his horse on
e heights at Austerlitz. It is possible to survey the sweep-
g moves and countermoves of two opposing armies on
e open plain below. Through the use of swift and com-
etent couriers, the general instructs his legions to ad-
nce here, to fall back there, to assault, retreat, entrap,
thrust and parry. From his position it is possible to pin-
oint the strengths and weaknesses of both factions and to
eploy his men accordingly. If he is swifter, craftier, and
ore ably understands the art of war, this general will,
arring untoward accidents, tend to defeat his enemy.
hese are also the principal tactics of backgammon. The
ame is conducted from offensive and defensive positions
f strength—or apparent strength—employing an intricate
lend of pace, balance and power. In short, it is the deft
nd deceptive art of being in the right place at the right
me and knowing how best to take advantage of it.

Try constantly to use your reasoning process. Often
e routine move may look good but in reality is weak.
rain yourself to anticipate, to realize that should you
ove one way, it will give the enemy a breathing spell,
hile another move may let him attack you where you are
ulnerable, so that this third and, at first glance, "wrong"
hoice may be the most intelligent.

All of backgammon's opening moves can be learned
y heart, but almost immediately thereafter both sides are

involved in the whys and wherefores of the game—ofte
after only the second or third roll. Tactics, then—what th
player intends to do in the game and how he intends t
control it—become very important at this early junctur
Some of the most interesting variations of early tacti
occur when one player throws a double on his openin
roll. For instance, in Diagram 39, red has opened with
4-2 and white has responded with double 4's. Red the
rolls a 3-2. Now, red does not want white occupying h
5 point, and so, in order to entice him from that point, h
moves a 2 from white's 12 point to his own 11 point, givin
white a direct 6 with which to hit him. He plays his 3 fro
his own 6 point to his 3 point. There are other alternative
of course, such as moving one man from white's 12 poi
to red's 8 point, but they are not as satisfactory.

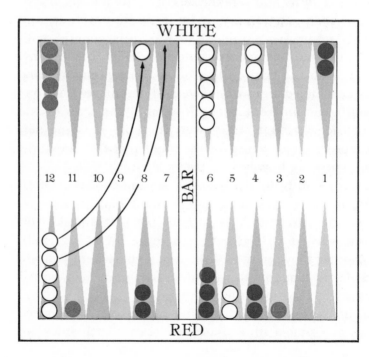

Diag
39

At this point, white rolls a 6-5, which would appear to
: an ideal roll. White can come off the 5 point now and
t red's blot, then continue on to his own 9 point. But this
ay would be incorrect. The 5 point is white's main de-
nsive bastion and he should not relinquish it lightly. The
:tter play would be to move one man from red's 12 point to
hite's 8 point and to start white's bar point with the 6.

This is the real beginning of backgammon; the game
no longer being played by rote. The impression of bold-
:ss in this play is deceptive; it is merely logical. Consider
hite's position if red now rolls double 1's or double 3's.
o play the 6-5 any other way, white would have too much
lose and too little to gain. If he were race-oriented,
almost all beginners are, hitting and moving on to
hite's 9 point would be his move, but this is not yet a
ce and it is a perfect time to leave a blot—especially
hen there is so much to be gained should red fail to hit it.
his is a good example of early imaginative tactical play.

In Diagram 40, white rolls an opening 5-1 and plays
correctly by moving one man from red's 12 point to his
vn 8 point, and dropping one man from his 6 point to his
point. Red then rolls double 4's, moving two men up
om white's 1 point to white's 5 point and two men from
is own 8 point to his 4 point. Red, of course, hits white's
ot on white's 5 point. White now responds with double
s. He comes in with one man on red's 1 point, and he
ops another man from his 8 point to his bar point, but
stead of covering it, he moves two men up from red's 1
int to red's 2 point. This move not only threatens red's
ot, but gives white a stronger defensive position. To
ver the blot on his bar point would be purposeless.
'hite's tactics are to lure red from his 5 point in order to
capture it himself. Red now rolls a 3-1 and makes his

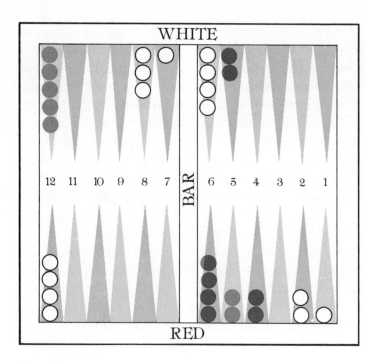

own 5 point by moving one man in from his 8 point an one man from his 6 point.

White, now in a weakened position, rolls a 6-5. Di gram 41 illustrates the correct way to play the 6-5. Whit might have covered the blot on his bar point, but again, would serve little purpose. The vastly superior play is t move two men—one from red's 1 point and another fror his 2 point—and establish a point on red's bar point. B doing this, white has exhibited a real grasp of the gam White should make this play under all conditions—in bot tournaments and money games. In this instance, red's ba is a stronger tactical position than his own. It is a pert nent example of early tactics and logic, and emphasizes th principle that in the early stages of the game your oppo

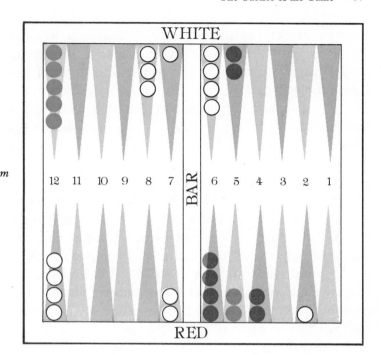

ram

ent's bar point is more valuable than your own, especially ʰhen the enemy holds an advanced point in your board.

The recurring leitmotif in backgammon is the ʳrength or weakness of the two 5 points. In this example, ᵈd has secured both of them, and white must do every-ᵗing in his power to drive his opponent off at least one of ʰem. To play the 6-5 in any other way is not only wrong, is craven. True, there are disaster rolls for white such as ᵒuble 2's or double 4's, but he has done the best he can ʷith his dice. More importantly, should those horror rolls ᵒt occur—and the odds, of course, are against them— ʰhite has secured a strong position without having ob-ᵗined either 5 point.

There are many crucial and constantly recurring situations in which beginners invariably make the wrong tacti cal plays. One of the most common is that of making you own 1 point too early in the game. The 1 point is ofte called the *guff* and is derived from the name of a man who though he otherwise played backgammon well, had an in vincible habit of making his 1 point in the beginnin stages of the game, or as soon as his opponent vacated th position.

Making the 1 point early on is almost always a wea and worthless play, and as a general rule, it should b avoided. It is the point of no return; if it is made too soor the men occupying it are out of play for the rest of th game. Moreover, should other points be open in your inne board, when your opponent is picked up and then enter from the bar, he is necessarily advanced. The 1 point is kind of limbo in which the men imprisoned there mus wait till the very end of the game before being borne awa to better things.

There is, to be sure, one important exception to thi general rule of thumb, which can arise, and often does, the very start of play. If your opponent, red, has rolled 6-4, 6-3 or 6-2 and moves one man from your 1 point int your outer board, or if he has split his back men, advanc ing one man to either your 2 or 3 point, and you then ro double 5's, the 1 point becomes much more attractive. I Diagram 42, you can see that it is now advisable to mov two 5's from your 8 point to your 3 point and two 5's from your 6 point to your 1 point. This aggressive tactic has es tablished two immediate points in your inner board an has hit at least one of your opponent's men (if red wa foolish enough to leave two blots in your inner board, h now may well have two men on the bar). As can be seen i the diagram, this play has given white three points in hi inner board, and if red fails to enter on his next roll, whit

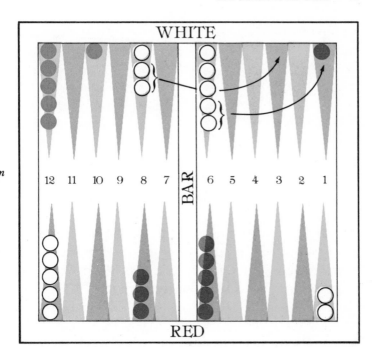

gram
2

as an excellent chance to win a double game. This is a good aggressive play and is the only exception to the general rule of not making your 1 point early in the game.

Another example of early tactical play is illustrated in Diagram 43. Red's reply to white's opening 5-1 is double 's, making both bar points. White then rolls a 4-2, making his 4 point and leaving a blot on his 5 point. Red now olls a 5-2. (The same general principle applies to rolls f 5-3 and 5-4.) Should red break on this roll—that is, hould he move one man from his opponent's bar point to is opponent's 12 point and the other man to his opponent's 9 point? Certain experts have suggested that in the elatively early stages of the game this is a sound and acceptable risk. But this is not entirely true. To begin with,

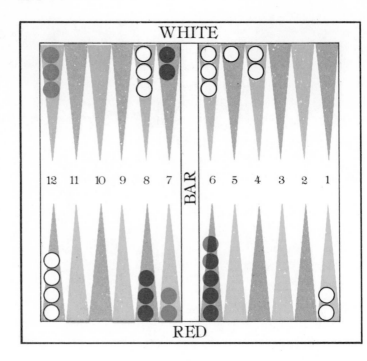

Diag
4:

in the early development of the game, your opponent's ba
point is extremely valuable. But there are other considera
tions. If red is ahead in a race and—more importantly—i
the weaker player, it would be sensible to run. Red is a dis
tinct favorite not to be hit (approximately 2¼ to 1 if h
rolled a 5-4, 9 to 5 with a 5-3 and 8 to 5 with a 5-2), an
should he escape, he has negated white's superior skill. I
red is ahead and escapes, he should double or, in a simila
position much later in the game, redouble if the doublin
block is on his side.* Every opportunity of this kind shoul
be grasped. White may, in fact, be a very slight underdo
in this position, but this is relatively unimportant whe

*See Chapter Seven for a discussion of the doubler.

he game becomes a straightforward game of dice. To fight he superior opponent on his own ground will probably entail complicated technical decisions in which the enemy has had more experience and hence a better chance to win.

These tactical moves apply, however, only when red is he weaker player. If red is the superior player in the above position, and even if he is ahead in a race, it would be folly to move his men from white's bar point. With the 5-2, red should bring a man from white's 12 point to his own 8 point with the 5, and start his 4 point with the 2. With the 5-3, he should make his 3 point with men from his 8 point and his 6 point. With the 5-4, he should move a man from white's 12 point to his own 4 point. You will note that red's blot, left after the 5-2 and the 5-4, can be hit by a 3, but this is not dangerous because, unless white rolls 3's and 1's specifically, he cannot hit red's blot and cover his blot on his own 5 point. Should white roll the perfect shot (hit and cover), it is still no disaster for red; he has three places to come in on his opponent's board (which makes him a 3 to 1 favorite), and he has that fine defensive point on his opponent's bar. The more experienced player always seeks involvement in order to implement his skills. In this position, to risk being hit is to give yourself up to the dice. In tactical plays of this kind, the abilities of your opponent invariably influence your play. What is sound in one situation is madness in another.

Another example of subtle tactical play occurs in Diagram 44. Red has opened with a 4-3, bringing two men down to his 10 and 9 points in attacking positions. White counters with double 2's, but instead of making the recommended opening play, correctly brings two men up from red's 1 point to red's 5 point in order to thwart red's two extra builders. Red then throws double 1's. In this instance, there is little point in red's making his bar point,

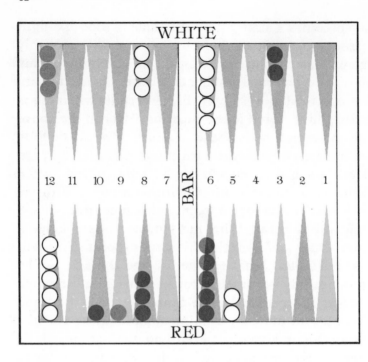

since white already occupies his 5 point. The sound tacti
cal play in this position is for red to ignore his blots and to
move his double 1's from white's 1 point to the 3 point
This is another illustration of a player attempting to lure
the enemy off his own valuable 5 point. It is true that red
is giving his opponent options, which under normal cir
cumstances he should not do, but in this situation he has
little choice. We realize that few players would make this
seemingly bold move, but not only is it the more conserva
tive play, it is also correct.

Here again, we can see that on only the third move of
the game, one of the players has a vital decision to make
and that this decision, even at this early juncture, could
affect the outcome of the game. Learning such early tac

ics is like learning the alphabet. Once he has learned
them, however, the ambitious player must then learn to
improvise, to juggle the letters in order to form more difficult and complicated word combinations. The opening
moves can be learned by rote; they are routine 99 percent
of the time. But immediately thereafter, both opponents
become involved in positions in which thought, deduction
and the imaginative exercise of tactics are of paramount
importance.

At first, such tactics appear more esoteric than they
really are, and if the beginner does not grasp their logic
right away, he should remember that they can be learned.
It is little more than the difference between learning to
walk and learning to dance. At some point subsequent to
learning the opening steps, a player, if he is to improve,
must learn to improvise and perform on his own. He must
learn the rules of the game and then deduce how and when
to break them, *since backgammon is all too often played in
contradiction of its own laws.* Thus, a talent for the game
presupposes a certain presence of mind, an imaginative
rendering of tactical detail, a knowledge of the specifics of
situations. In short, as Clausewitz said of war, "It is the
power to discriminate, rather than the readiness to general-
ize."

◄ 4 ►

BASIC ODDS
AND PROBABILITIES

All action in war is directed on probable,
not on certain, events.
— *Karl von Clausewitz*

A knowledge of the odds
and probabilities is essential to backgammon. They are no
difficult. Most beginners look upon the odds as a kind o
mathematical hocus-pocus and turn away, as from a
strange and somehow frightening fog. But this is usuall
because the figures have been presented to them as some
thing complex and difficult to learn. If you are particularl
adept at mathematics, this knowledge will help your game
but a rudimentary grasp of simple arithmetic is all that i
basically required. Most of the odds and probabilities in
backgammon could be learned in a day by any normall
bright ten-year-old.

Should these assurances be insufficient, we would lik
to point out that we know several backgammon enthusi
asts, some of whom would qualify in the semi-expert class
who either refuse to learn the odds for the usual obstinat
reasons, or are just too indolent to care. Though thei
games would be much improved if they took the time t
learn the percentages, the fact remains that they hav

chieved startling success without them. But these are the xceptions; normally, a knowledge of the odds is essential the game.

The important thing to remember at the start is that these odds are so simple and logical that mathematical misfits have been known to learn them in a surprisingly short time. Ignore the fact that hitherto math has been anathema to you and concentrate briefly on the following paragraphs. We do not intend a complicated lecture; rather, we will direct your mind to the natural logic of the game. Backgammon is basically a game of logic upon logic upon logic, like a series of simple children's blocks.

To begin with, there are two dice for each player. You are concerned with only two at a time, either yours or those of your opponent. Each die has six sides, numbered from 1 through 6.

Now, when rolled, two dice produce any one of only 36 combinations. No more: just 36. Regardless of how many times you roll the dice, you will never roll more than 36 combinations. You would agree that this limits the study considerably. What are these 36 combinations? If the dice show any specific double—as, for example, a 2 and a —this is one of the 36 combinations. Therefore, rolls of 1-1, 2-2, 3-3, 4-4, 5-5 and 6-6, the only possible doubles, account for 6 of the possible 36 combinations, leaving 30 others. If any two different numbers appear when the dice have been rolled—a 2 and a 1, for example—this roll will account for 2 combinations. Why 2? Well, a 2 on one die and a 1 on the other is one combination. But would it not have been possible for the 2 to have been a 1 and the 1 to have been a 2? Since both of these combinations must be included, whenever you roll two different numbers they count as two different combinations. Therefore, adding up all of your possible rolls—excluding, for

the moment, doubles — you would have the following com
binations:

1-2	2-1
1-3	3-1
1-4	4-1
1-5	5-1
1-6	6-1
2-3	3-2
2-4	4-2
2-5	5-2
2-6	6-2
3-4	4-3
3-5	5-3
3-6	6-3
4-5	5-4
4-6	6-4
5-6	6-5

Note that the sum total of these is 30, which, added
the 6 doubles, makes a grand total of 36 different possib
combinations of the dice.

Now, if 1-1 has one chance out of 36 of being throw
how many other rolls are there that might have a
peared? The answer, of course, is 35. Thus, since the
is only one 1-1 and 35 other possible combinations,
it not logical and ridiculously transparent that the od
against rolling a 1-1 on any and all individual rolls a
35 to 1?

We have pointed out that any number which is not
double constitutes 2 combinations. What, then, are th
odds against rolling a 6-5? There are 2 combinations th
produce the 6-5 (6 on one die and 5 on the other, or 5 o
the first die and 6 on the second), and 34 that do not (sin
the 2 combinations subtracted from the 36 possible rol
are 34). When reduced to its lowest common denominato

ιe fraction $^{34}/_2$ is $^{17}/_1$, so the odds against rolling a 6-5 on ιy specific roll are exactly 17 to 1. (Incidentally, if you ιve ever visited the Las Vegas casinos in order to play ιaps, you may recall that they will offer you only 14 to 1 ι exactly the same proposition, one of the several reasons ιey are unlikely to go broke.)

Now the first key formula is established. A roll of 1-1 ιas been shown to be a 35 to 1 shot and 6-5 a 17 to 1 shot. *ou now know the exact odds of every combination that two ιce can possibly show.* Not only double 1's but all other ιecific doubles are 35 to 1, and not only 6-5 but all other ιmbinations, excluding doubles, are 17 to 1.

As mentioned in Chapter Two, the most often used action in backgammon is 25 to 11. Try to remember this ιespite the fact that it seems an odd, lopsided number. *h*y 25 to 11? You are already equipped to understand the ιswer.

This figure represents the exact odds against you ιhen you have a single shot at one of your opponent's ιlots. For instance, let us assume that your opponent is ιearing off and has a closed board except for a blot on his ι point. You are on the bar, and only a roll of a direct 4 by ιou can hit it. How many of the 36 combinations on the ιce will produce the 4?

$$
\begin{array}{ll}
 & 4\text{-}4 = 1 \\
4\text{-}1 & 1\text{-}4 = 2 \\
4\text{-}2 & 2\text{-}4 = 2 \\
4\text{-}3 & 3\text{-}4 = 2 \\
4\text{-}5 & 5\text{-}4 = 2 \\
4\text{-}6 & 6\text{-}4 = \underline{2} \\
 & \phantom{6\text{-}4 =} 11
\end{array}
$$

Eleven rolls will hit your opponent's blot, and the ιemaining 25 rolls will not. Thus, the odds against your

rolling a 4 are 25 to 11. Extending this formula, the od[
against rolling any specific number are again exactly ;
to 11.

Try to grasp the logic behind these basic computation
If you do understand everything we have discussed so f
in this chapter, you are well on your way to learning virt
ally all you need to know about the purely mathematic
aspects of backgammon. Of course, the game is muc
more than plain numbers, but here we are interested sp
cifically in basic percentages and probabilities.

You now know that *any* time you have one direct sh
at one of your adversary's open men, regardless of wh
that shot is—a 1, 2, 3, 4, 5, or 6—you are a 25 to 11 unde
dog. That is, he is approximately a 2¼ to 1 favorite not
be hit. But now let us assume you have a 4 to hit and the
are no intervening checkers between your man and hi
Are you able to calculate your exact chances of hittin
Since you have the tools, try to work it out before readir
further. But do not be dismayed if you fail; it cannot be r
iterated often enough how comparatively simple this who
chapter will become when you have thought it through.

You have already learned that there are 11 chances
roll a direct 4. To that you must add those numbers th
total 4 on *both* dice; these are 1-1, 2-2 and 3-1. Sin
3-1 comprises two shots and 1-1 and 2-2 are one apiec
there are a total of four extra chances, which you must ac
to the original 11—making a total of 15 chances. If 15 rol
hit, how many miss? Subtracting 15 from 36 (the tot
number of combinations), you get 21. The odds, the
against you are now 21 to 15, or exactly 7 to 5, which
much better for you than 25 to 11.

Assume that you have one direct shot, which as yc
know by now makes you a 25 to 11 underdog. The percer
age figure here is 30.55. This is determined by taking tl

vorable chances—11—and dividing them by the total
umber of rolls: 36. If you are a 25 to 11 underdog, you will
it 11 times and miss 25 in 36 games over the long run—
:, put another way, you will hit 30.55 times and miss
).45 in 100 games over the long run. Any percentage
gure can be determined in this way. If you are a 3 to 1
nderdog on a specific roll—there are 27 chances against
)u to 9 in your favor—you can discover the percentage
gure by dividing 36 (the total number of rolls) into 9 (your
.vorable rolls); the result is 25 percent, or one chance in
)ur—which is to say, 3 to 1. You will hit 9 and miss 27 out
f 36, or hit 25 and miss 75 out of 100 if you are a 3 to 1
nderdog. These "percentage" figures seem superfluous to
s, but are mentioned here in case the reader finds them
asier to comprehend.

You can always work out this kind of problem right at
ie table. You need only to count accurately, and when the
ptions arise, make sure that the percentages work in your
ivor and not in that of your opponent. It goes without say-
ig that the more often you calculate these percentages,
ie easier it will become. If you are comparatively new to
ackgammon and never have been much interested in
dds, you now have all the information you require to se-
·ct the best percentage move. Take your time, count up
ie shots, compare your choice with your alternatives and
ien make the play that is most in your favor.

Superstition and hunches play a large part in crucial
ackgammon decisions. This is all right as far as it goes
id is not entirely to be sneered at, but be sure you don't
:t your superstitious whims defy percentages. Assume, for
cample, that you have arrived at a critical position in
hich you are forced to leave a blot, and it is vital for you
ot to be hit because your opponent has a closed board.
ssume also that you have a choice of leaving your blot

where it can be hit by a 1 or by a 6, including all th
combinations (2-2, 3-3, 4-2, 5-1) because no men inte
vene. You have a strong feeling that your opponent
going to throw a 1 on his next roll, and your hunc
shrieks, "Don't leave him the 1!" Yet there would t
grounds for having you committed if you followed th
whim and left your man open to being hit by the 6 instea
of the 1.

Follow these intuitions only if they are even or bett
percentage plays than any alternative. Never follow the
in defiance of the odds, no matter how strongly you feel.

When any decision has to be made, always attempt t
eliminate the guess. A simple, workable formula to app
is to play percentages at all times and to follow whateve
hunches occur to you only when the odds are precise
even. A simple, logical approach to backgammon does n
mean that you will always win, but you will lose less ofter

When you are on the bar, the chances of entering you
opponent's board are the other important fundament.
odds of backgammon. When you are on the bar and you
opponent has a one-point board—probably his 6 point—th
only roll on which you cannot enter is a 6-6. Wheneve
your opponent has a one-point board, you are a 35 to 1 fa
vorite to come in. But should he make just one mor
point—any point—the odds are reduced to 8 to 1. Th
explanation is relatively simple. Suppose your adversa
has his 6 point to begin with and a short time later als
makes his 5 point. Now 6-6, 5-5 and 6-5 (which, as note
earlier, also counts as 5-6)—that is, a total of four shots
will block you from entering. Four shots are bad for yo
and therefore 32 are good, so the odds are 32 to 4, or 8 to
in your favor.

If three points are covered, the odds against you ar
naturally reduced further; they are now only 3 to 1 in you

vor. And if four points are covered, they are reduced still further to only 5 to 4 in your favor. When your opponent has established five points in his board, you are for the first time a distinct underdog, in this case, 25 to 11 against.

The important thing to remember about this is that you must learn not to be frightened of your opponent's board, since it is only when he has established five points that you become an underdog to come in. It is also something of a consolation to know that even if he has established a five-point board, you are still a very slight favorite to enter in two rolls. What is called *entry failure* is a niggling annoyance for everyone. But the next time you are on the bar bemoaning your fate, remember that you are always a favorite to come in unless your opponent has a five-point board, and even then you are a slight favorite to enter in two rolls.

In essence, these are the basic odds of backgammon, and as you have seen, they are neither complicated nor shrouded in that impenetrable fog. If you will spend a little time to master the figures discussed in this chapter, you will be equipped to handle virtually all the problems of the game's percentages.

This subject has been simplified intentionally. It would have been possible to delve more deeply, to discuss the subject in terms of higher equations and negative probabilities, but this kind of approach is unnecessary. In bridge, for instance, if a player is well versed in the fundamentals of the game but has never learned how to bring about a crisscross squeeze, his game is only minimally affected because the odds are that it will come up only once or twice in a lifetime. Similarly, in backgammon you now have all the basic mathematics you need in order to play the game well.

THE ODDS ON ROLLING UNOBSTRUCTED NUMBERS

1: 25–11 against
2: 2–1 against
3: 11–7 against
4: 7–5 against
5: 7–5 against
6: 19–17 against
7: 5–1 against
8: 5–1 against
9: 31–5 against
10: 11–1 against
11: 17–1 against
12: 11–1 against

THE ODDS ON ENTERING WHEN A MAN IS ON THE BAR

With a five-point board: 25–11 against.
With a four-point board: 5–4 in favor.
With a three-point board: 3–1 in favor.
With a two-point board: 8–1 in favor.
With a one-point board: 35–1 in favor.

◄5►

BEARING OFF

The Policy employed in waging war
troubles itself little about final
possibilities, but confines its attention
to immediate probabilities.

— *Karl von Clausewitz*

Bearing off is a science in
self and worth more than the casual study that players
ormally devote to it. As explained in Chapter One, when
ny of the points in your inner board are held by your op-
onent or when any of his men are on the bar, the object is
▷ bear off your men with a combination of speed and safety.

Let us assume that white has a closed board, and that
ed has a reasonably good inner board and a man on the
ar. The optimum position for white is shown in Diagram
5. Of course, the problem is different when your opponent
ccupies any of your points — that is, bearing off is more
ifficult — but let us first examine the less difficult position.

In this optimum position, white is a strong favorite
ot to give a shot — that is, to bear off his men without
⸱aving a blot. As he bears off, he continually attempts to
eep his high men even. For example, should white have
⸱ree men on his 6 point and two men on his 5 point, a roll
f double 6's or double 5's or 6-5 would leave a man ex-
osed. This kind of position should be avoided whenever

possible. In such situations, your critical point is alway
your highest point or two points, and you should strive t
keep it or them even.

Given white's optimum position in Diagram 45, bea
ing off is a relatively uncomplicated procedure—thoug
even here it is never certain that you will not leave a blo
Still, it is the safest position at which to aim when bringin
men into your inner board prior to bearing off.

The possibilities of being hit increase, of cours
when red has established positions on any of white'
points in white's inner board. In such an event white's ta
tics will change—in some cases, deliberately violating th
basic rules of bearing off. For instance, in Diagram 4(
where white occupies red's 1 point, red has already born

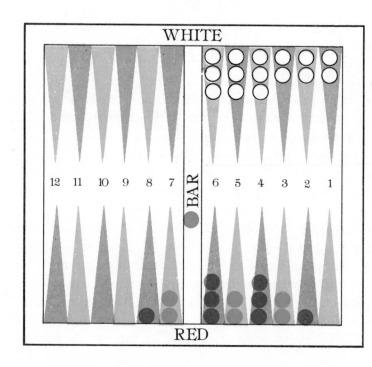

Dia
4

f three men and has a 1 to play. If red moves his 1 from
is 5 point to his 4 point, subsequent rolls of double 4's
r a 5-4 will leave a single shot (blot), and the horror roll
f 6-5 will leave a double shot. If, however, red moves his 1
om his 3 point to his 2 point, he has broken the cardinal
ile of keeping his high men even and has made himself
ulnerable to the potentially disastrous rolls of 6-5, 5-4,
-3, 5-1 and double 6's, or four extra single shots, but no
ouble shots. Which is correct? Against White's prime we
ould move down from the 5 to the 4 point, risking a
ouble shot. But were White's board no threat, play from
e 3 to the 2 point, guaranteeing not to leave two men
ulnerable. If red had had a closed board with white on
e bar, there would be no question about his moving his 1

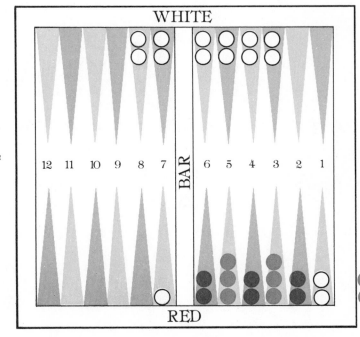

gram
6

from the 5 point to the 4 point, since there would be n
number that could hurt him in this position. To repea
your options of play are always dictated by your opponent'
position.

Diagram 47 illustrates an example of play in bearin
off that seems to contradict all the percentages. White ha
a closed board and red, who has already borne off five mer
now rolls a 5-3. If played strictly according to the percen
ages, the correct and apparently reasonable play would b
to bear off one man from the 5 point and move the othe
man down to red's 2 point, thereby giving white only
one-shot, the odds of which are 25 to 11 against. In orde
not to be hit, this in fact is the correct percentage play. O
closer examination, however, there is more to this positio

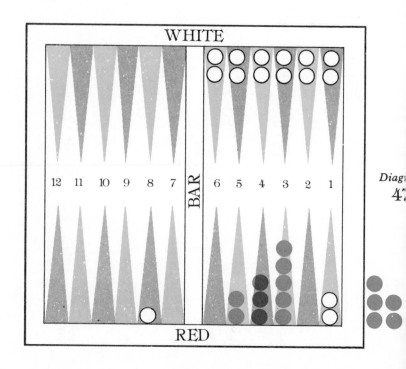

Diag
47

han percentages. If he is not hit, red's next roll is fraught
vith danger. Any high number which is not a double, such
s 6-5, 6-4 and 5-4, will give a double shot. Double 3's
lso will give a double shot, and any roll that does not in-
lude a 1 or a 2 will leave at least a single shot. The rec-
mmended play, therefore, is for red to bear off two men —
ne from the 5 point and another from the 3 point. By
oing this, red is taking a calculated risk. In addition to
he direct 4, this gives white two other shots (3-1 and 1-3)
t red's blot on the 5 point — odds of 23 to 13 against, but
etter than 25 to 11. Taking two men off, moreover, gives
ed seven men off altogether, bringing him to just below
he *break-even point* of nine men off. (For an explanation
f the break-even point, see p. 83.) But the main reason for
naking this play is that if red is not hit, his next roll has
nany more chances of being safe , for regardless of what
e rolls, he cannot leave a double shot; thus, it is the better
lay

This is a good illustration of fluid reasoning. A good
eneral principle to follow is that if you must leave a blot
vhich, if hit, could cost you the game, it is best to leave it
vhere, according to the percentages, your opponent is least
ikely to hit it. Yet because of other attendant factors, it is
est to contradict the principle in this particular position.

In Diagram 48, white, who has no men off the board,
olls a 5-4. He bears off his 5 and now has an option of
laying one of two 4's. There is only one correct way of
laying this move. If white takes a man off the 4 point, he
an be hit with a 4 or a 3. If he moves a man from his 6
oint to his 2 point, he can be hit with a 4 or a 5. In each
ase, the odds of being hit are exactly the same: red is a 5
o 4 favorite to hit. But if white plays the move correctly —
y moving a man down from the 6 point — and red then
ails to hit him, on white's next roll he is a solid 8 to 1

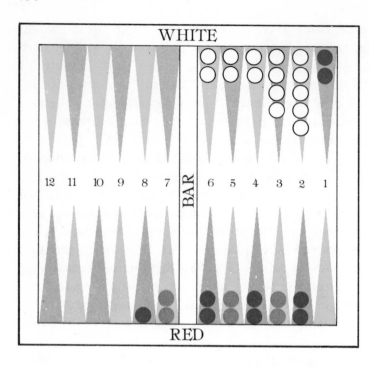

favorite not to leave a blot. The only bad shots are doubl
5's and 4's, and 5-1. Had white played his 5-4 the othe
way—by taking two men off—there would have been 1'
rolls which left blots, and in some cases two of them
White would now be only a 19 to 17 favorite not to leave ε
blot—much less than 8 to 1. The principle involved here i
always to leave your blot high up rather than in the middl·
of your board if possible. If you are not hit, your next rol
will be easier to play.

Diagram 49 is an example of a principle that man
players, particularly beginners, tend to forget. In this posi
tion white, with four men off, has rolled a 5-2. Many nev
players would move the 5 from the 6 point, hitting red oı
the 1 point and move a 2 from the 4 point to the 2 poinı

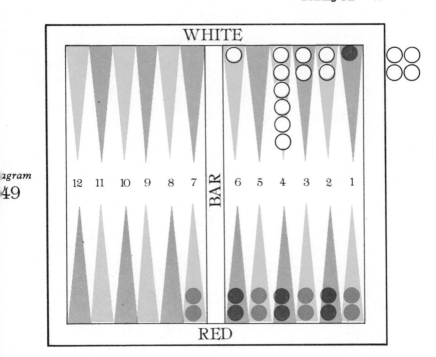

Diagram
49

They forget that the roll can be played in two ways; either number may be played first. Thus, the correct tactic is to move the 2 from the 6 point to the 4 point and then to take off the 5. Playing a 2-5 when bearing off in this position saves white from leaving an unnecessary and dangerous slot.

Again, a paradox. One might easily believe that this principle always applies, but in the following instance, in Diagram 50, it is again more advantageous for white to break the rule. In this position, white has four men off and now rolls a 6-1. The 6-1 should be played by bearing off the 6 and moving the 1 from the 4 point to the 3 point. If he makes the recommended move, white's bad subsequent rolls are double 6's, double 5's and double 4's. But if he

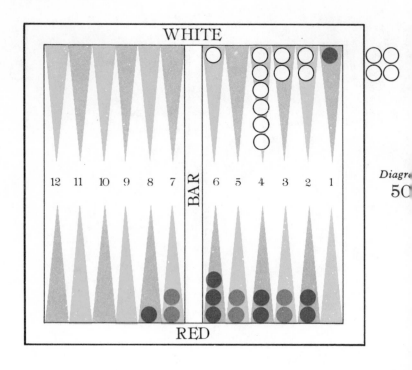

Diagr
50

simply takes the man off the 6 point and leaves six men or
his 4 point, he will be vulnerable to a 6-3, 5-3, 4-3 or
2-3, so he will have eight potential bad rolls instead of
three. Furthermore, should the horror roll occur—that is
double 6's, double 5's or double 4's—white will still have
nine men off, and if his blot is missed, his double-game
potential is strong.

In Diagram 51, white has borne off four men and now
rolls a 4-3. In this case, white is going all out for a double
game. Red is a 5 to 4 favorite to come in. White gains
virtually nothing by bearing off two men in this position.
He should take a man off the 4 point and move the odd
man on the 4 point down to the 1 point. It is safer, and if

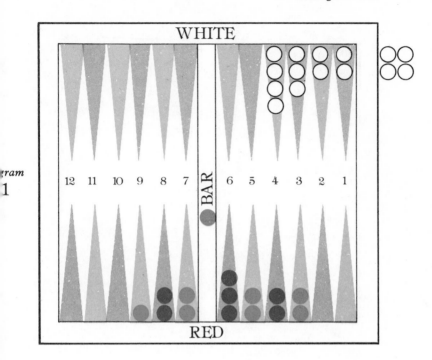

ill still take him the same number of rolls to bear off all
is men. (We are assuming, of course, that no doubles will
 thrown.) Only double 3's, double 4's, double 5's and
 uble 6's hurt him; even if he rolls them, he will have
 ine men off and consequently will still be a favorite to
 in if red hits his blot. Of these doubles, incidentally,
 uble 3's are the worst, since, if white plays them correct-
 — that is, as safely as possible — he can bear only two men
 ff.

In Diagram 52, red has borne twelve men off and
 hite now rolls a 6-1. Here again, the correct play is to
 ontradict all our principles and to bear one man off the 6
 oint and another off the 1 point, leaving two blots. It is

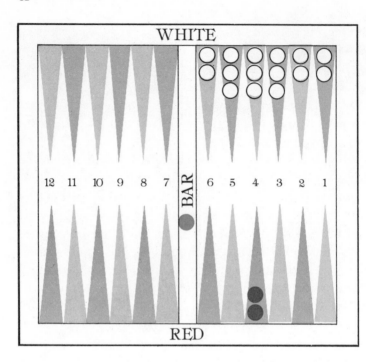

not played this way because white *wants* to be hit. It is ju
that it is very much to white's advantage to be hit *if* r
rolls a 6 or a 1. Were the blot on the 6 point not there, ar
red rolled a 6, the game would be virtually over, since re
would be a prohibitive favorite in this position. But if th
blot on the 6 point is hit, white has an additional opportu
nity of coming in and hitting red again as he comes aroun
to his home board. More importantly, if red now rolls a
without an accompanying 4 or 5 or 6, he will have to brea
his position in his inner board with any 1, 2 or 3, thereb
giving white the unexpected opportunity of being able t
capture all three of red's men and winning the game easil
Lastly, if red fails to roll either a 6 or a 1, then white is tw
men nearer victory.

This is one more example of your opponent's position rcing you into contradicting all the principles you have therto learned. It is a position which demands the des-:rate gamble, since without it all will be lost anyway.

A few basic percentages: If white, against red's closed)ard, is hit while bearing off, the *break-even point* in terms ' his winning is somewhere between eight and nine men f. In other words, when white has borne off nine men, he a slight favorite to win, but with only eight men off, : is a slight underdog. However, we would recommend \at white accept a double* if he has borne off at least six en, provided that all the rest of his men are positioned ı his lower points. This recommendation is made on the ·emise, explored later, that if you are a less than 3 to 1 ıderdog, in the long run you will gain by accepting the)uble. If white has borne off all his men but two, and they e on the bar, he may also accept a double, since he is :rtainly less than a 3 to 1 underdog.

When bearing off, if red, for example, has a closed)ard and white has borne off all his men except one hich is on the bar, white is between a 13- and 14-to-1 fa-)rite to win.

Further, when red has a closed board and is attempt-.g to win a double game, he should not pick up too many ' his opponent's men along the way. A safe number of en to capture would be four. This is an important safety ctor. The more men white has on the bar, the longer it ill take him to come in, and hence the more chances he ill have of hitting red while red is bearing off.

The preparation of your board for bearing off—that is, e immediate positioning of your men just prior to bear-

ee Chapter Seven on the doubler.

ing off—involves tactics of some importance. It has bee
suggested by certain experts that in a race you must g
your men into your home board as quickly as possible
order to bear off more rapidly. Generally this is true, b
since backgammon is replete with sly paradoxes, there a
occasions when it is not, and to operate on that princip
all the time would be costly. For example, in Diagram 5
red rolls double 1's. In this instance it would be folly
use the double 1's to bring the lone outside man into red
inner board. The correct play is to move two men from th
6 point to the 5 point, one man from the 4 point to the
point and one man from the 2 point to the 1 point. Red
still behind, but his position is considerably improved.

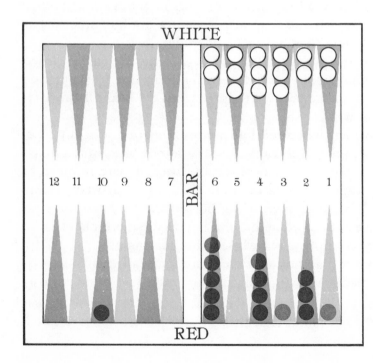

Diag
5

inging the one man in, on the other hand, red would,
hen bearing off, be wasting all rolls of 5's and most rolls
 3's and 1's, and would fall even further behind. To make
e point more pragmatically, if red were to bring the lone
an in and white then doubled, it would be an almost
npossible *take* (acceptance of the double); played the rec-
nmended way, if white doubles, red should take it.

A further guideline about coming in: generally speak-
g, it is wiser to start the high points rather than the low
ints in your inner board. The only time to start the low
ints is for diversification, when you have made the high
es already. In a race, when coming in, try not to leave
ps in your inner board. As discussed above, it is usually
good practice to employ 1's for this purpose rather than
 advance your outside men.

In Diagram 54, white has borne off twelve men. Red
as a 1 to play and is trying to save (avoid losing) a double
me. Sometimes the playing of a simple 1 is essential to
e's basic strategy, though many players seem to feel
at because the roll moves so short a distance and wields
 apparent power, it is unimportant. Nothing could be
rther from the truth. The example shown in Diagram 54
 indicative of this. By playing the 1 correctly here, red
creases his chances of saving the double game by exactly
0 percent. It is a good example of how subtle the playing
 1's can be and how careless play can penalize the unob-
rvant player. Many players, nearly resigned to losing the
uble game and believing the movement of the 1 to be
latively unimportant, would move it from white's 10
int to the 11 point in order to move that much closer
me. But by so doing, they have limited themselves to
ly two rolls that could save them: double 4's and double
s, a 17 to 1 shot. Had they left the outside man where it

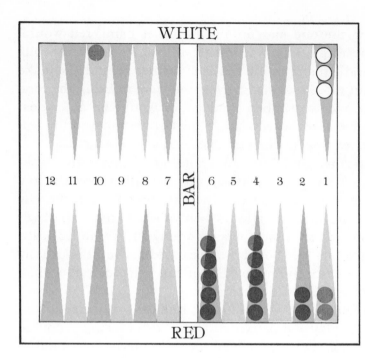

was, however, and moved a 1 from red's 4 point to the
point, double 5's and double 3's would also have saved tl
double game. Red would now be only an 8 to 1 underdog
assuming, of course, that white did not throw a doub
himself. As is evident from this and countless other exai
ples, the deployment of 1's can be crucial in general ove
all tactics.

Diagram 55 is another example of the important u.
of the 1. In this instance red has a 1 to play before whi
rolls. Here again the 1 is enormously important. Assumir
again that white will not roll a double, if red moves his
from the 6 point to the 5 point, he becomes a 19 to 17 f
vorite to bear both men off on his next roll (there are l

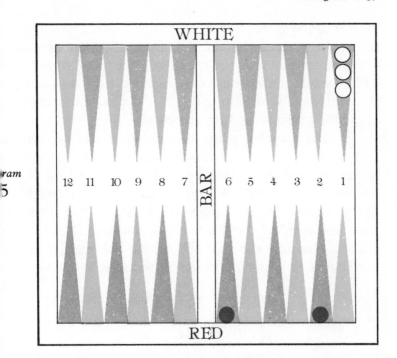

mbinations which will bear off a 5-2). But if he moves
e 1 from the 2 point to the 1 point, he will be a 21 to 15
iderdog to bear both men off (there are only 15 combina-
ns which will bear off a 6-1).

If a bookmaker could get 19 to 17 on one side of a
oposition and 7 to 5 (the same as 21 to 15) on the other,
: could retire within a month. This situation actually
curred in a tournament: a player moved the 1 from his 2
int to his 1 point, and when his adversary had completed
s next roll, bearing two men off, red then rolled a 6-1
win the game. His adversary was justifiably perturbed,
ough he refrained from saying so. A roll of large doubles
red would have been less disturbing, since doubles are

built into the game, but to make the wrong move and the
throw the perfect number to win is a flagrant example
why backgammon is the cruelest game. Red won *becau*
he had made the wrong move, and because he won, he b
lieved it was the right move, and it is doubtful that anyor
could have persuaded him otherwise.

In Diagram 56, white has already borne off five me
and now rolls a 2-1. In this instance, two men should I
taken off. Red is a 3 to 1 favorite to come off the bar. I
bearing two men off, white saves an entire turn because I
has an even number of men left. It is well worth the ris
Bear one man off the 2 point and another off the 1 poir
This contradicts the rule of keeping the high men eve
but increases white's chances of winning a double gam

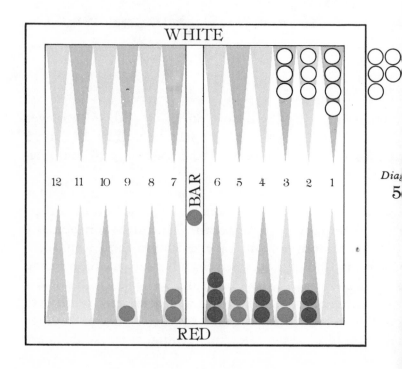

Dia

5

nd at this moment—before he has rolled—red is more
an a 17 to 1 underdog to hit.

In Diagram 57, the position is only slightly changed.
/hite has one more man on his 1 point, but because of
is, white's strategy also changes. Here white has nothing
› gain by taking two men off, as he did in the previous
iagram. By doing so, he leaves himself in a position of
naximum exposure without having achieved any tangible
:wards. In this instance, white should bear off one man
om the 3 point. Admittedly, he is still open to being hit if
:d fails to come in and he then rolls any double except
ouble 1's. Even so, at the moment, it is over 90 to 1
gainst red hitting white; even if he does, white will have
orne off a minimum of seven men (if he rolled double 2's)

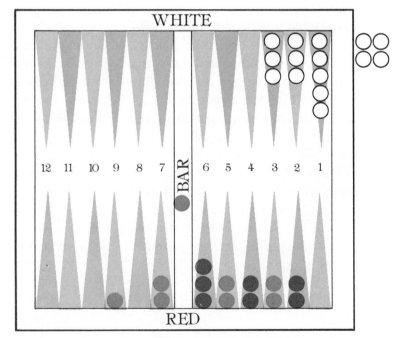

ram
7

and with any larger double, he will have borne off nine men

Unlike the play in Diagram 56, white should not take two men off in this position. We do not object to bold, courageous play; we do deplore plays that make no sense. Bearing two men off does not improve white's position any way. The reason for the difference between the two plays is one of simple mathematics. If white had taken two men off in this position, he would have created 20 extra chances to leave a blot on his next roll, and if red failed enter he would have been offered a gratuitous opportunity to hit and win the game. White would have gambled foolishly because he had nothing to gain. To take it a step further, if white had had a mathematical certainty of winning a double game—if, say, red had six men in his outer board instead of three—the obvious correct play would be to play it perfectly safe and move a man from the 3 point and a man from the 2 point down to the 1 point. Again, white's play is influenced by his opponent's position.

Here, as in all other aspects of the game, success is predicated on sound deductive reasoning. We cannot advocate strongly enough that the player think rather than simply push his men about the board. Backgammon is a game of calculated risks. By bearing men off in the recommended way, you have risked a subsequent horror roll of doubles. Why? To hurt yourself? No; because it improves your position. You leave a blot intentionally. Why? Because you have calculated that the potential rewards are worth the risk and that you stand to gain much more than you will lose. This is the essence of backgammon: the ability to assess the different and sometimes difficult choices confronting you.

◄6►

THE BACK GAME

Defense in itself is a negative exercise,
since it concentrates on resisting the
intentions of the enemy rather than being
occupied with our own.
—*Karl von·Clausewitz*

The first general and important axiom concerning back games is that they should be avoided. More often than not, the back game is a rearguard action thrown up to resist the inevitable flood. It can be a colorful and exciting tactical play; it can be brilliantly executed and even rewarding, but in the main, the back game has too many sudden pitfalls, too many built-in snares, to be viable more than half of the time. To begin with, the back game requires meticulous timing and is comparatively easy to defend against by an experienced player; and when disaster strikes, as it is wont to do, even the expert is vulnerable to losing a double or even a triple game. (In England, the back game has a better winning percentage, since triple games are not recognized there.) The timing is so critical that if certain horror numbers are rolled, they can destroy the back game completely. The back game is not a happy place in which to find yourself, and its devotees are reminiscent of the little Dutch boy with his finger in the dike.

If you must play a back game, however—and often

there is little other choice — the principal tactic is to esta
lish at least two fortified positions in your opponent's i
ner board. To occupy points in your opponent's board
tantamount to invasion, an occupation of enemy territo
not with a view to keeping it, but as Clausewitz said
occupied enemy territory, "in order to levy contributio
on it." The preferred points to occupy are the low ones
the 1 and 2 points, the 2 and 3 points or the 1 and 3 poin
The ideal positions are the 1 and 2 points, but only if y
have perfect timing. However, it is almost always diffic
to time your game perfectly, and in practice the occupati
of these two points also tends to stop the enemy from pla
ing 5's and 6's as he is bringing his men in. It is bett
therefore, to attempt to establish the 1 and 3 points, c
failing that, the 2 and 3 points.

Having accomplished this, it is to your advantage
have as many of your men hit as possible. This is partic
larly true if you have established three points in your opp
nent's inner board. In such a case it would be to your a
vantage to have all fifteen of your men distributed on the
three points. Your opponent would be unable to comple
his board and none of your men would be out of play or
any danger of it.

Meanwhile, in your own inner board, you must nev
attempt to establish forward points — that is, the low
points. They are ineffectual and out of the action. It
much like establishing a forward position when the re
war is being waged behind you. Above all, it is importa
to establish the higher points in your own board, maintai
ing other men behind them as a kind of mobile reserve
order to make up the rest of your board effectively.

In its essence, the back game is backgammon play
in reverse. It is a series of tactical maneuvers which
against all the player's natural aggressive instincts. It is
game in which the defender prefers to be hit and hopes f

w numbers rather than high. It is a game for masochists.

The back game can occur quite accidentally right at ṭe outset. In Diagram 58, for example, red had an open-ṇg roll of 4-1 and played one man from white's 12 point ṭ his own 9 point, and dropped one man from his 6 point ṭ his 5 point. White responded with double 4's; using one ṃan from red's 1 point he hit red twice, and with two men ḟom his 8 point he established his own 4 point. Red then ọlled double 3's, a great shot, entering two men and mak-ṇg his own 5 point, and, as illustrated in the diagram, af-ṭr only three rolls finds himself immersed in the entangle-ṃents of a back game. Like a man suddenly set upon by a ọg, red's tactics are now almost exclusively defensive.

In defending a back game, you must try not to help ọur opponent by hitting his open men. More importantly,

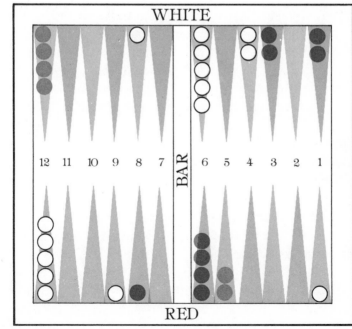

gram
ṣ8

and particularly if his timing is right, you must allow your
self to be hit, especially when he has no blots in his boar
He will attempt to leave as many blots there as possib
since, if you are hit, you may be forced to hit him agai
thereby giving him another man in your inner board. A
lowing your own men to be hit gives you the necessa
delay and may destroy his timing. But this is a matter
some cunning and tactical maneuvering.

Some of these principles are illustrated in Diagra
59. In this position, red rolls a 6-3. Most players in th
situation would move their man on white's 5 point out
white's 11 point and move the odd man on their own 1
point to their bar. This illustrates the difficulty of learnin
the theory inherent in the back game. The play that shou
be made is to slot the man on white's 10 point on red's

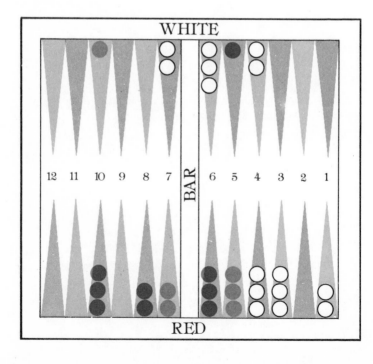

Diag
5

point, and to move the man on white's 5 point out to white's 8 point. The reasoning behind this tactic is as follows: If white does not roll a 5 or a 6 on his next roll and does not hit your blot, he will have to move forward in his inner board, which he would prefer not to do. Then if red rolls a 1 or an 8 on the next roll, he can cover his open man, thereby restricting white's movements to his own inner board and probably destroying it. On the other hand, if white does roll a 5 or a 6 and hits red, this will give red more time in which to preserve his semi-prime. This is a battle of masochists, since both red and white long to be hit in order to be delayed for as long as possible. White has a beautifully balanced back game, but ultimately he will have to break his anchors on red's 3 and 4 points or destroy his inner board. Red has a fine semi-prime and should strive to maintain it for as long as he can. That semi-prime is not only red's main offense, his spearhead to safety, it is also his chief defense, since it prevents white from releasing his reserves. Oddly enough, white's position would be much improved if his seven remaining men were on the bar. He would, in fact, be in a better position to win the game.

This is another example of the game's paradoxical nature. Two contestants are attempting to mobilize their men around and off the board as speedily as possible, and yet are making moves calculated to slow them down — and both sides are perfectly correct in doing so. But every back game has its built-in potential for self-destruction and it could easily be set off in this position. In this same diagram (#59), suppose white now rolled double 4's. Unable to escape from red's board, he would be forced to tear down his own. Should red then roll a 1 or an 8, white would be sealed in and the remnants of his inner board would be destroyed. Hence, white's position here, though not hopeless, is not auspicious.

Diagram 60 illustrates a back game which has reache
the critical point for both factions. Disaster rolls coul
destroy either position. The worst roll for white is doubl
3's; for red it is double 5's. This, of course, is the chie
drawback to back games; regardless of the painstaking pre
cautions both sides have taken, they are now each in a po
sition where one roll could initiate a landslide. It is tha
tense moment when both armies, having thrown them
selves into the fray, now wait for signs that indicate whic
side will falter, break and melt away.

At this point, however, white rolls a 5-2. The roll i
not as unfortunate as it appears to be. White's mandator
play is to move the 5 from the bar point to the 2 point an
the 2 from the 6 point down to the 4 point. Paradoxicall
white's main strategy is not to advance his men in his in

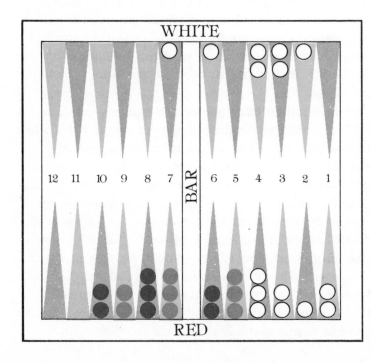

Diag
6(

:r board. He does not want to establish forward positions.
nd yet to accomplish this, he must move his men down
far as they will go. This tactic saves him from being
rced into playing 5's and 6's, gives him breathing space
id allows him to delay. At this crucial moment in the
ime, when victory could turn either way, it would be to
ich player's advantage to have his opponent roll. They
e both employing, or would prefer to employ, delaying
ctics.

One strength of white's position is that he has created
ree points in red's board. On the next roll, should red be
rced to break his prime by rolling high numbers, so that
s opponent will subsequently have to play from either
e 3 or the 4 point, white will still command the 1 point
id either the 3 or the 4 point. Assuming that eventually
hite retained only the 1 and the 3 points, but was forced
break one or the other of them, his position would be
ntamount to three soldiers defending their position
;ainst an enemy battalion. But with three points secured
, they are in the diagram, white's position is not nearly as
id as it looks. As it is, the game is nearly even, although
d must be slightly favored because of the threat of the
)uble game. If white had a four-point prime in red's inner
)ard, his first tactic would be to break it so that red would
: able to play. In this instance, the open 2 point permits
d to play any 6, which otherwise he could not do. It is a
:licate situation. The only real reason for white to have
»ur points in red's inner board would be if he had all fifteen
' his men distributed on them. White would then be an
verwhelming favorite to win. As it stands, however, the
de of the game could turn either way.

In Diagram 61, an illustration of the classic back-
ime position, white rolls a 2-1. He has three options, the
ost advantageous of which is to bring one man from red's
point to red's 3 point, and to move the outside man from

the 10 to the 11 point. It would be unwise to hit the bl
on red's 2 point, thereby following the general rule f
back games of not hitting, but maintaining a strong defe
sive position. If white did hit, however, which many pl
ers would tend to do, he should then, rather than movi
the outside man, move a man from his own 3 point to l
1 point—giving red 3's, 2's and 1's on which to come
and hit. In this position, white prefers to be hit. But shou
red then roll 4's, 5's or 6's, white's campaign strate
will have been thwarted and he will probably not be at
to save his board because he is much too far advance
Even should red roll his worst possible number, a 1-5,
would remain in a formidable position. The whole theo
and practice of the back game is illustrated here. Howev
if white played correctly—that is, not hitting red's blot

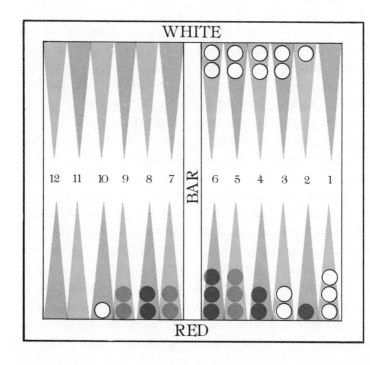

Dia

6

2 point — he is hardly worse than even money to win the ame. White's tactic is to force red to play. By hitting, he is abotaging himself. Incidentally, having four points in his wn inner board is a complete illusion of strength at this age, and white should not place much faith in it for the oment.

There are, however, no moves in backgammon where trocious plays at certain times cannot become "correct" a result of subsequent happy rolls. In chess, for exam- le, if white made a foolish play tantamount to hitting d's blot, he would be forced to resign within a few oves. But given the curative powers of the dice in back- ammon, the stricken player could well be saved. For in- ance, suppose that white actually hits red and then oves his outside man up two points. Red then rolls a 1- , coming in on the 1 point and electing to move a man , breaking his 9 point. Suppose, further, that white en rolls a 1-6, moving from red's 2 point to hit red's ther blot. Red then rolls another 1-5 and is forced to ome in on white's 1 point and to move another 5 from his point to his 2 point, as is illustrated in Diagram 62. ed's game has become a disaster, and in light of the re- ults it would be difficult, if not impossible, to convince hite (or most fortuitous winners) that he had made the rong play. Yet such accidents happen all the time.

Most of the basic principles of the back game are illus- ated in Diagrams 61, 62 and 63. In Diagram 63, red, hav- g held on to white's 1 and 2 points with six men, man- ged to time his game perfectly, and after white had borne ff twelve men he finally got a shot and hit white's blot n the 3 point. Two rolls later, white rolled a 6-1 to enter d's board and leave it. The position is illustrated at this oint. Up to this moment red's back game has been per- ctly timed and played, but he still has a long way to go. is problem is not only to catch that lone man of white's

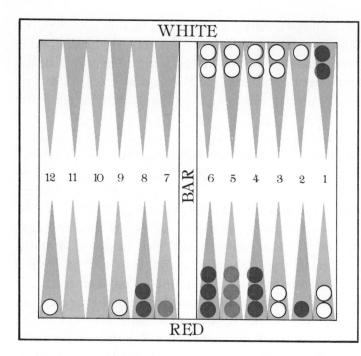

WHITE

12 11 10 9 8 7 BAR 6 5 4 3 2 1

RED

Dia

6

outside, but, if possible, to capture another man, since th
is his best chance to win.

Red now rolls a 4-3.

Most players are taught that in situations of the bac
game's aftermath, they should diversify their men in ord
to give them a broader base of attack. But unless a block
established somewhere, white's two men on his 4 point a
immune to any red assault. The correct play is to move th
two men from white's 7 and 8 points up to form a block o
white's 11 point. By doing this, red is, in fact, devious
attacking those men. Of course, red could block doub
6's, double 5's and double 4's (although double 5's wou
be to red's advantage, since it would leave two blots; mor
over, with double 4's, red is still a favorite to hit). Ther
fore, by blocking white's 7's, red has made a more practic
and far more imaginative play. Now any roll of white's t

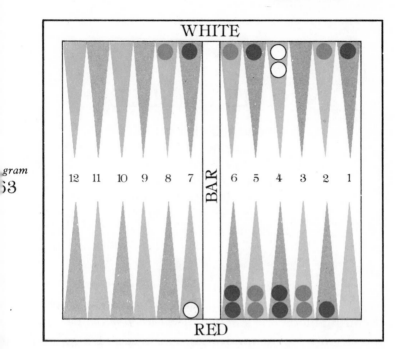

gram
53

ling 7 will force him to break the block on his 4 point. It
s 5 to 1 against that white will roll a 7, but if he does, red
an double and white should drop.

Variations of this situation occur frequently in back
ames and should be looked for. Again, such plays are en-
irely a matter of imaginative use of tactical positioning.

It is important to study the intricacies of the back
ame and not to be cowed by their complications. You
nust learn to comprehend the reasoning behind such tac-
ics as opening up, hitting and not hitting, blocking and
ot blocking, and the delicate timing factor; otherwise you
vill always be at a clever opponent's mercy. Given the en-
anglements of this type of game, however, and the fact
hat more often than not it leads to at least a defeat and
ften a gammon, it cannot be stressed strongly enough
hat, whenever possible, back games are to be avoided.

◄7►

THE DOUBLER

Capitulation is not a disgrace.
A general can no more entertain the idea
of fighting to the last man than a good
chess player would consider playing an
obviously lost game.
—*Karl von Clausewitz*

The introduction of the doubling block (variously called the *cube* or the *doubler*) a relatively recent innovation and has added an extraordinary new dimension to the skill of backgammon. The importance of astute use of the doubler is, in fact, difficult to exaggerate. Should an expert player from Armenia, for example, where they do not use the doubler, compete against an average player who is expert in its use (if there is such a phenomenon), the latter would win. The doubler is the key to backgammon.

The doubling block is a large die with numbers ranging from 2 to 4 to 8 to 16 to 32 to 64. At the beginning any game, this die rests at the side of the board and brought into play by whichever player thinks he has the first advantage. Either player may double or redouble only when it is his turn to roll, and only *before* he rolls. For example, if one player believes he is ahead at any moment in a game being played at 10¢/$1/$10 or whatever a point he may double his opponent to 2. (Without the doubler

ae point is scored for winning a single game.) Either
ayer may make the first double, but having done so, he
ay not double again until redoubled by his opponent. If
e opponent wishes, he retires, or declines the double,
ereby losing 1 point—or 10¢, $1 or $10. If he accepts,
owever, the stakes are now at 2, or 20¢, $2 or $20, and
ould he find himself ahead at a later stage in the game,
e may double back to 4, thus increasing the worth of the
me to 40¢, $4 or $40 if his opponent accepts it.
ncidentally, just because the last number on the die is 64
oes not mean the doubling stops there. Theoretically, the
egree of doubling is unlimited and can go on to 128, 256
l2, and so on, though in an expert game the doubler rare-
 rises above 4. The reason for this is the respect expert
ayers have for the doubler.)

Further, occasionally at the beginning of a game, both
ayers, rolling one die, may roll the same number. By
ior arrangement, the doubler may then begin at 2. These
e called automatic doubles, but they play no part in the
rategy of backgammon, nor are they ever used in tourna-
ents. They are only employed in certain money games as
means of increasing the stakes.

A volume could be written on the doubler alone. As-
ame, as so often happens, that someone shows you a cer-
in backgammon position and then asks: "Should red
ouble and should white accept?" Given this scant infor-
ation, the question is meaningless. In order to answer
e question accurately, one must also know who is play-
g whom. Is it a tournament match, and if so, what is the
ore? What are the relative skills of the opponents? Is it a
oney game? Is red redoubling or is this the first double?
ow high are the stakes? Is it a chouette, and if so, how
any players are involved? These are just a few of the fac-
rs that must be clarified in order to answer the question.

The longer one considers the doubler, the more co[m]plex it seems to become. Does your opponent tend [to] take doubles? If so, wait until his position is nearly hop[e]less. Is he prone to dropping early? Then offer hi[m a] double against the odds in the hope that he will. He[re,] as in other areas of backgammon, adapting your gam[e] to your adversary's is vital. The taking of a double agai[n] player A would be a certain drop against player B. Y[ou] should double player C early and be more cautious agai[n] player D. More often than not, the unobservant play[er] merely examines the position on the board. For instan[ce,] if white doubles red in the situation in Diagram 64, r[ed] with a block on white's 5 point, and white with seve[n] men still to transport into his inner board, red should [ac]cept if white is the stronger player, whereas he shou[ld]

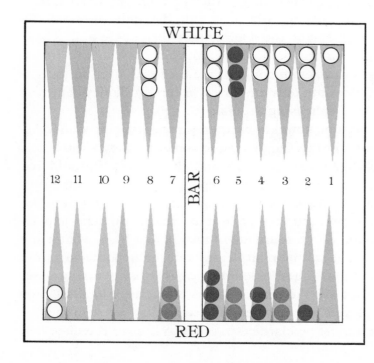

Dia[gram]
6[4]

op if red is an expert pitted against a weaker player,
ice there is little expertise left in this game. The dou-
er is a razor-sharp boomerang and it could be suicidal
 allow it to fall into the wrong hands. Therefore, the
ving of a double depends not only on the position of the
oment but on the psychological make-up and technical
ility of your adversary.

To comprehend the theory inherent in the doubler is
obably the most important part of backgammon. The
rifty use of this instrument can launch an ordinary play-
 into the higher echelons of the game. Beginners are
variably taught not to take "bad doubles." Of course the
vice is sound and sensible, but there is a corollary which
 even more sensible: Do not drop when you should take.
*nquestionably, the greatest number of points lost in back-
mmon is by players refusing doubles they should have
ken.* One should not take bad doubles, but a more
·sitive philosophy is: When in doubt, take. Consider
e fact that if you take four doubles and lose three of
em, you are still even — presupposing, of course, that no
mmons are involved. This phenomenon will be exam-
ed later in the chapter; for the moment, accustom your-
lf to accepting playable doubles. Few players understand
e leverage they acquire by taking a double. By doing so
d by not redoubling until the right moment, you are in
e game to the end. Even if the roof falls in, you can still
ke advantage of every miracle roll to extricate your-
lf.

Generally speaking, then, when do you take a double?
you are less than a 3 to 1 underdog and there is no dan-
r of losing a double game, you should take a double
ery time in money games. It may seem odd to allow the
ikes to be doubled when you are an underdog, but con-
ler the logic of the matter. Assume the stake is $1 a

point and you are doubled by your opponent. If you dr
you lose $1. If you take the double, you risk losing o
additional dollar—that is, $2. On the other hand, if y
win the game, you *win* $2. Thus, your net position, inste
of being −1 (if you had refused the double) is now +2
difference of 3. So by taking a double and winning, you
$3 better off than you would have been if you had dropp
You have won $3 while only risking one additional doll
Therefore, any time you are less than a 3 to 1 underdo
you should accept a double.

In Diagram 65, white has two men on his 2 point a
red has two men on his 1 point. All their other men ha
been borne off. At this point, white doubles. Should r
accept? In money games, the answer is yes, yet time af

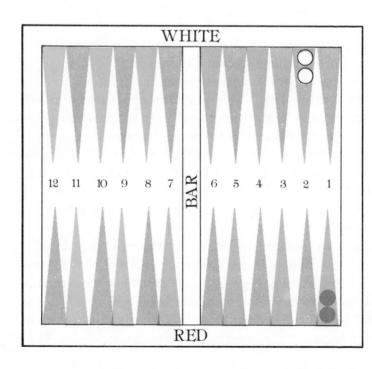

Dia
6

ne people drop in this position. Sometimes a player will
, "I'd take if I were being doubled from 2 to 4, but not
en it's from 32 to 64." This kind of specious reasoning
cowardly and exasperating. If it is a take from 2 to 4, it is
st as much a take from 32 to 64. How many combinations
es white require to bear off both men on this roll? The
swer is 26. All 1's except double 1's prevent him from
ming off—a total of 10 unfavorable combinations. Thus,
e odds are 26 to 10, or 13 to 5, in favor of white. The frac-
n 13 to 5 is less than 3 to 1, and since red is getting 3 to 1
r his additional dollar, he should accept. This is a basic
le of thumb for accepting doubles. On the other hand,
iite is perfectly correct in doubling, since he is a 13 to 5
orite to win. Here is an example where one player
ubles, his opponent takes, and both are correct.

Obviously, to want to double the stakes, you have to
ahead, but it is a matter of opinion just how *far* you
ould be ahead. In our opinion, if it is possible to com-
te, you should be at least a 3 to 2 favorite when you offer
e first double, but you should be a minimum favorite of 2
1 to redouble. The reason for this discrepancy is that
fore the first double is offered, the cube is in the public
main; that is, either player has access to it and may em-
oy it. But once you have been doubled, the cube becomes
ur property and can never be taken away from you. It is
e most potent weapon in your arsenal and you should be
iry of releasing it. You should wait, in fact, until you are
irly certain that your adversary will capitulate.

There are occasions when your position becomes
erwhelmingly powerful within a few moves and the op-
rtunity for a gammon arises. In this case, do not dou-
e—unless your opponent has a point in your inner board,
which case you should double him out.

In other words, avoid playing for a gammon (usually

in tournaments and almost always in money games) if yo
opponent has a block on your 1 point and a potenti
board—that is, when he has no men out of play. Th
holds true regardless of how many of his men you have
the bar. You are in jeopardy until the game is over, not
mention the jolting psychological blow of losing a har
fought game at the eleventh hour. The enemy is too apt
get one or more shots before the game ends. Here the ri
rarely justifies the rewards.

One of the persistent curiosities of the doubler is th
if you refuse a double in three consecutive games and a
right twice and wrong once, you are losing money. This
proved again and again in chouettes, where one player
pitted against two or more players, and where it is oft
possible to witness the outcome of a game after you ha
dropped. Consider (assuming, of course, no gammons):
you drop three times, you are −3. If you had taken all thr
doubles, you would be −2, −2 and +2, for a net of −2, o
point better off than those who dropped all three games
But it is difficult to convince someone who has just be
right two out of three times that he is wrong. Wrong he
however, and the sooner he understands it, the wealthier
or less poor—he will be.

A few general random rules

If you have accepted a double, and, later on in t
game get a direct shot (25 to 11 against) which, if you h
will win the game for you, the acceptance of the doub
has been vindicated. (Again, this presupposes no gar
mons.) In the long run, your take will have been justifi

---

*There is an interesting psychological factor at work here, which will be d
cussed in Chapter Eleven.

en if in this specific instance you do not hit the blot. his is just another way of saying that you were less than 3 to 1 underdog, since 25 to 11 is approximately 2¼ to 1.

Let us assume that you have borne off several of your en, but in doing so leave a triple shot. If your opponent isses, he is in great danger of losing a double game, but : doubles anyway. Most players look at the triple shot as ough they had seen a ghost; they blanch and drop. But ey should take. The odds are 3 to 1 in your opponent's vor, which you will remember is the dividing line for king doubles; therefore the take per se is even money. ut you have an excellent chance for a double game if ur opponent misses, and so what you stand to gain by king makes it, in effect, a winning proposition financially.

Regarding "late" doubles: A moot position often aris- in a chouette (discussed in detail in the next chapter) hen some members of the partnership wish to double the x and others do not. Assume the final decision to be not double. The captain then rolls a perfect roll, destroying s opponent's position. Those who had advocated dou- ing now complain that it was wrong not to have doubled fore, when the box would have accepted. On the next ll the captain doubles, the box drops, and recrimina- ns multiply.

Two important factors are generally overlooked in ese situations. The captain could not have known that : was about to roll the perfect shot; in fact, the odds were ainst it. More importantly, by waiting one roll, the part- rs now have the money in their pockets, whereas if they d doubled earlier and it had been accepted, the box uld still be in the game with a chance to win. Any time u can force your opponent to drop, you have accom- ished a great deal. More than anything else, the dice e to be respected, for they have all the power. By dou-

bling and making your opponent surrender, instead
merely raising the stakes, you show your respect for th
dice and sever their hold on the outcome of the game.

   If the doubler is on your side and you roll a sh
which turns the game around so that you will be able
redouble on the next roll, you must be sure to take no in
petuous risks with any part of that roll. Do not give yo
opponent an opportunity to roll the perfect retaliatory sh
In Diagram 66, white has a 5-1 to play. Given the fa
that the doubler is on white's side, the correct play here
to move from red's 3 point to his 8 point, hitting his bl
and to move the man from white's bar point to his 6 poir
This play thwarts the potential miracle rolls of 1-6 ar
5-2 by red. For regardless of whether or not red comes i

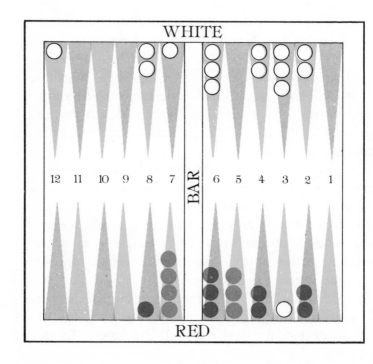

Diag
6

ite is ready to redouble on almost all return rolls by red,
d does not need to take any risks. To save the 1 is not
wardly; it is using the doubler to win the game. You
uld make this play if the doubler was in the middle or
your side. On the other hand, if the doubler is in red's
rner, white should make his best tactical play—that is,
hit red's blot and to use the 1 to make his bar point,
ereby giving red only a 5-3 to hit. Because white cannot
e the doubler to knock red from the game, the duel will
won or lost on the field; hence, white must make his
st tactical maneuver. Here again it can be seen how the
ubler influences the action, circumscribes one's choices
d dictates the way in which the men are moved.

In Diagram 67, red has been doubled and owns the

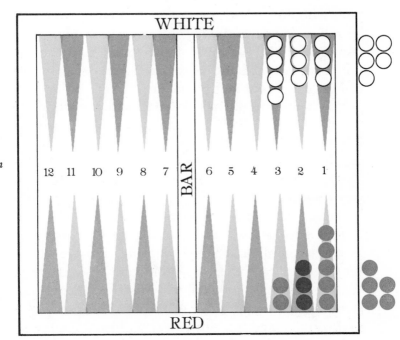

*am
7

cube. The game develops into a race, and both playe
reach a position where they have five men off and the oth
ten distributed more or less equally on their 1, 2 and
points. But it is red's roll. Does red redouble? Not yet. It
true that red is ahead in a race, and if no doubles a
thrown, he will win. But if red releases the doubler no
and white rolls a double and red does not, white can redo
ble and red will have to drop.

A sound rule to follow about redoubling when beari
off: If both players have five rolls left (that is, ten men p
sitioned on the lower points), wait. You may consider r
doubling with four rolls left, depending on your opponer
and you must *always* redouble with three. If both playe
are left with six men—which is three more rolls—and yo
redouble now, your opponent has no equity in owning th
cube. Let us say you roll and take two men off. Now
rolls a double, taking four men off. You still have a chan
to roll a double and win, and since it is not his turn,
cannot double you out of the game beforehand. Thu
when each combatant has six men remaining on the low
points, the redouble is mandatory.

If neither side has doubled and the cube is in th
middle, you may offer a double much earlier, since you a
giving up no equity. If you can calculate that there are se
en rolls apiece remaining, offer the first double immed
ately. The redouble, however, is another proposition;
that case you are trying to double your opponent out of th
game, not to double the stakes.

In advocating "takes" as a general winning philoso
phy, we should issue one warning. Beware of the cor
pletely emotional take to which many players are vulner
ble. In chouettes, for example, over the years we have see
dozens of players join the game late. The box will offer a
early double and the new player will examine the positio

ien drop, though he is no more than a 7 to 5 underdog in
ie game. The chouette continues and the new player hits
bad streak and falls behind. At this point he gets into the
ox, becomes involved in a hopeless position and is open
o losing a double game. He is now offered a double by his
pponents and accepts.

This kind of neurotic take is suicidal, deserves to be
unished, and usually is. When deciding whether or not to
ake a double, remember to analyze each position, each ac-
eptance or refusal, on its merits alone. Ignore the score in
money game and try to estimate whether or not you are a
to 1 underdog or less, with no double-game dangers. If
his is the case, accept the double; if it is not, regardless of
ow you feel or how lucky you believe your opponent to
iave been, drop and get on with the next game.

To sum up: When in doubt, take; when in doubt, do
ot double. In backgammon, it is better to be a taker than a
iver.

Though not included in the official laws of backgam-
non, there is another wrinkle to the use of the doubler, in
vhich one contestant may *beaver* his opponent—provided
oth parties have agreed beforehand to allow beavers. In
his further refinement the player who has been doubled
iot only has the right to accept, but immediately, *before*
iis opponent rolls, may redouble and *retain* the cube.
Thus, if player A doubles player B to 2, B can accept and
edouble to 4 before A rolls, yet still retain the right to
edouble to 8 whenever he wishes.

This addition is colorful and escalates the gambling
ngredient, but in an expert game you will hardly ever see
i beaver being offered. By itself the single take will be
:nough, because the expert knows what he's doing and
vill not offer a rash double.

The Use of the Doubler in Tournaments

When you sit down against any opponent, always hesi
tate when he offers you the first double—unless it's a clea
take, in which case you should accept so gleefully that i
may make him unsure of himself. But if you're going t
drop, don't hurry. Look over the board, regardless of th
position, and appear to consider taking the double. I
bridge such a ploy would be unethical, but in backgam
mon and poker this tactic is completely acceptable. Doin
this creates the impression that you hate to drop (which
on principle, you should), and so your opponent will ten
to be more cautious in the future about increasing th
stake. As a result, you may get a free ride for several roll
later on, during which you may throw the miracle roll tha
turns the game around.

Whatever else may be said of it, the doubler is a partic
ularly lethal weapon in tournament play, where it can ac
tually favor the weaker player—if only he recognized it
power and knew when and where to exert it. Not long ago
for example, a comparative beginner drew an expert in th
opening round of an important tournament. It was a 15
point match, the score was 6–3 in favor of the expert
In the next game the expert gave the beginner an earl
double, almost expecting him to drop because *he* had dou
bled. But the beginner was not so easily cowed; he accept
ed and the doubler was now at 2 on his side. The gam
continued, swinging back and forth, and several moves lat
er, one of the beginner's men was captured and placed o
the bar. The expert, white, had a five-point board, but ha
a blot on his 4 point, as well as two additional blots in hi
outer board. The beginner had managed to construct
prime, as is illustrated in Diagram 68.

As the beginner (red) prepared to roll, he was mor

an a 2 to 1 underdog (25 to 11, to be exact) to come in
n white's 4 point. But had the beginner thought of it,
here was a clever doubling tactic to be employed in this
osition. Even though he is the underdog, it is imperative
hat he now redouble. In order to overcome the expert, he
ill have to win this game; thus he must double against
he odds. In this position the expert would prefer not to
e doubled. If the beginner rolls a 4, he will deal the
xpert a stunning psychological blow; he will almost cer-
,inly win 8 points, and the match will be in jeopardy.

This is just one example of how a beginner can use
he doubler to compensate for his opponent's superior
chnical abilities. If the beginner fails to hit the blot, he
ill fall behind 10 – 3 or possibly even 14 – 3. But if he hits,

gram
8

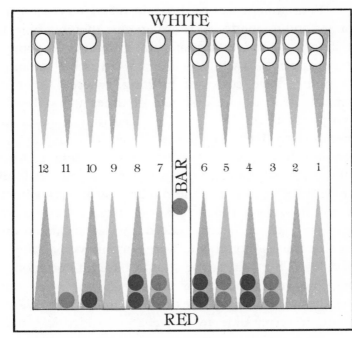

the score could be 11−6 in his favor. It is an immens
opportunity and should be taken; in the parlance of base
ball, it is not a time to bunt, but to hit away. (Needless t
add, were the positions reversed, an expert would be mos
inexpert were he to redouble here.)

Whether or not the tyro hit the blot is irrelevant. Th
point is that like so many others in similar positions, h
failed to recognize his opportunities. The thought of re
doubling never crossed his mind.

Situations of this kind occur repeatedly in tourna
ments, and the inexperienced player tends to be too timi
or too naïve to capitalize on the leverage he has in th
doubler. Of course the doubler is a two-edged threat, bu
the beginner can make use of it in a way no expert woul
consider doing. He must learn to recognize and then t
snatch these major opportunities.

Tournament tactics differ in many ways from mone
games and chouette. In tournaments, the only objective i
to defeat your adversary, and the difference in your score
is immaterial; to win 15−0 or 15−14 is the same. Thos
14 points have cost you nothing, whereas in a mone
game, you would be charged 14 times the stake. Let u
assume that you have an 11−1 lead in a 15-point tourna
ment match. Early in the next game, your opponent has
remote chance, should everything go right for him, c
winning a gammon. In the tournament you would drop i
he doubles, remaining ahead 11−2; in money games, yo
would take every time. The strategies of the two types c
play are vastly different. Indeed, the tactics are so dissimi
lar that it is as though you were playing with a different se
of rules. This vital factor should have an enormous effec
on how you handle the doubler during your differen
matches. At different times in the same match in a tourna
ment, it is possible to arrive at two identical position

hich, in the one case, you would drop if doubled, and in
ιe other you would take.

A familiarity with the numerous complexities of the
:rawford Rule is essential, and it is surprising that so few
layers trouble themselves with this crucial adjunct to
ιurnament play.

The Crawford Rule stipulates that in, for example, a
5-point match, when one player reaches 14 and his oppo-
ent has a lesser score, the player who is behind may not
ouble in the first subsequent game. When that game has
een completed, however, he may then double at will.
'his rule applies each time one player is a point from vic-
ιry; it is used in American tournaments, but not as yet
broad. The Crawford Rule is an attempt to protect the
layer with the greater score, but in our view it does not go
ιr enough. A fairer rule would be one that prohibits your
pponent from winning more points than you can poten-
ally win in any one game. For example, in a 15-point
ιatch, if player A is ahead 1–0, the most player B could
ʹin in the next game would be 14. If player B is ahead
0–7, the most player A could win would be 5, and so on.

The difference in tactics when the Crawford Rule
; in use is complicated and far-reaching. Suppose that
ou are playing an opponent just as skillful as you are,
nd the score is 13–13 in a 15-point match. What will
ɔur doubling strategy be in this crucial game? Should you
ouble early, late or neither when the Crawford Rule is in
ffect? The answer is that you should tend to double ear-
er than usual, because you give up no leverage; that is, he
as no advantage in owning the cube, since if he accepts,
 will be the last game and there is no point in redoubling.
econdly, he is almost forced to take the double, since if
e drops, he must win the next two games (barring gam-
ιons) to win the match. Therefore, by doubling you have

reduced this match to a one-game proposition, in whic you have a slight edge — obviously correct tactics.

The only time you should not double in this situatio is if there is an inkling of a double game. In this case, yo must go for it — of course taking every precaution not t lose a double game yourself. This latter strategy applie whether the Crawford Rule is in effect or not.

But in the exact same situation — that is, a 15-poir match which is drawn 13 – 13, and no Crawford Rule your doubling tactics are altogether different. There is n redouble here either, but in this instance your opponer has nothing to gain by accepting the double. Therefore h would drop and double you at the beginning of the ne game. Your best tactic in this situation is to go all out t win a double game and the match — again attempting to er sure that you do not lose a double game yourself. Your fir priority, then, is to set up a defense to prevent that poss bility. Having accomplished this, you must try to secur the gammon, even at the risk of losing a single game.

In this situation, at what point *should* you double The answer, regardless of the strength or weakness of you position, is "almost never." If you double and he drops, yo have won nothing, for the 1 point you have won is useles Being ahead 14 – 13 only gives you the dubious privilege c dropping on the next game after the opening roll, whe your opponent will certainly double you.

There is one specific exception to this rule. As is ev dent in Diagram 69, red is vulnerable to losing a gammo and the match if he does not hit one of white's two blots. H has been in danger of losing a double game throughout, bι now he unexpectedly finds himself a 5 to 4 favorite to wi the match if he doubles. Since red will in all probabilit lose a gammon if he misses, he has nothing to lose here b doubling. He might just as well lose 4 as 2, since eithe

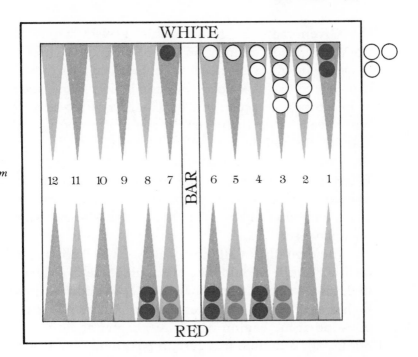

am

ss will cost him the match. This is the kind of situation which the thoughtless player will not consider a double, nce he is so relieved at the possibility of saving a double me, but this is specious reasoning. Failing to double at is critical juncture is a deplorable blunder; it is tantaount to losing by default. This is his opportunity to win no extra risk to himself; therefore red must double.

White's tactics in this game have been absolutely corct. He has been going all out to win a double game, and nce he has three men off, he now cannot lose a double me. Therefore he is able to play as recklessly as he nooses — unless red thwarts his plans by doubling, there-• putting him in danger of losing the match, from which : has hitherto been exempt. It is a marvelous moment r the bold and unexpected counterattack.

Given red's crushing double, should white take
not? It depends entirely on the respective abilities of tl
players. If white is clearly the better player, he shou
drop, since in this special situation he is a 5 to 4 underdo
If he drops, the score will be 14–13 against him, but I
will have a better than even chance in the next game. WI
should white allow himself to become an underdog whe
he is the favorite? But if white is much the weaker playe
he should take, since at the moment he is only a 5 to
underdog, whereas if he dropped, he would be much mo
of an underdog in the next game, given the superiority
his opponent.

Incidentally, in all money games, if red doubles in th
position, white should take every time. He is only a 5 to
underdog, which is less than 3 to 1, in addition to whic
he has excellent gammon expectations. You may recall tl
question at the beginning of this chapter about whether
not to take a double in a certain position. This is a perfe
example of that decision being dependent on many diffe
ent factors. In one case, you take; in the other, you drop
and in both cases, the position is exactly the same. This
just one more indication of the kind of fluid reasonir
backgammon requires.

The kind of reasoning and logic involved in the pr
vious example will, if heeded, improve your game in a
departments. It is worth remembering, since even exper
are wont to overlook the subtleties of the doubler. In a r
cent tournament, two of the world's top players, tied at 9
9 in an 11-point match, reached the position in Diagra
70. In this position, red doubled and white took. Not on
was it an atrocious take, it was an even more atrociou
double. It is difficult to determine which player exhibite
the greater folly. This is another example of translatir
your prerogatives from one context to another. In a mon

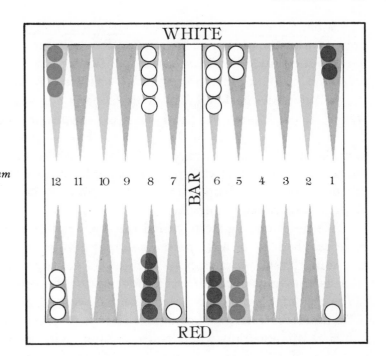

ram

)

me, this is a definite take, but in a tournament with this
ore and no Crawford Rule, the position must be seen in
different light, since different tactics now apply.

If white drops, he has lost 1 point, which means next
nothing. True, he has given his opponent a free drop
ee next page) on the next game after the opening roll,
it this is a minuscule edge compared with the benefits
gains from dropping here. Since in the next game he
ill double at once and put the match on the line, to take
e double in this dodgy position is absurd. And what does
d gain by doubling? He assumes that white is going to
op, and so anticipates gaining one point. What red should
ve done in this position was to go for the double game.

What actually happened was that white took the do ble and won the game and the match. Red was furious t white's ineptitude had been rewarded. White, having wo defended his take, insisting that *his* was the correct pla

White was challenged by a third party for a sizal wager; he could, said the third party, pick five independe experts, and if any *one* of them agreed with white's de sion, he would win the wager. After much waffling, wh backed down. This is yet another example of how a pla er's ego can obstruct his reason, causing him to justify arrogant and indefensible play.

We mentioned a tactic called the *free drop*. When y have reached 14 in a 15-point match and your oppone has some lesser *odd* number — such as 5 — you may util what is known as a free drop. If your opponent opens wi say, a roll of 3-1 and you now roll a 5-2, you should dr if he doubles. There is no logical reason to play out t game in this position when you must play with even t smallest of handicaps. Dropping does not significan affect the score, and given the respective opening rol your position is now inferior to his. The reason why t score is not particularly affected is that your opponent st requires the same number of victories to win the match. 14 – 5, and assuming he doubles on the first roll of eve game, since he loses nothing by doing so, he requires fi victories in order to reach 15 and to win. At 14 – 6, he st requires five victories to reach 15. You must learn to u this free drop at your first opportunity. Most players kno enough to do this when the score is 14 – 13, but you c apply the same principle to any odd number. However, t number must be odd; it would be madness to let your o ponent run from even to odd. Thus, dropping in situatio of this kind is an excellent tactic to employ.

Tournament play is replete with sly conundrums th

not exist in money games. Hence, tournament play
demands not only different skills, but more exacting ones.
For example, when you reach 14 in a 15-point match with
the Crawford Rule in effect, it is always preferable to have
your opponent at some lesser odd number. You *prefer* him
be odd. Conversely, if the final goal is an even number,
you want him at an even number. But the reverse is true
when the Crawford Rule is not in effect. Whether your
opponent's score is odd or even will not alter your strategy
any great degree, but it is worth knowing whether you
want your opponent at an odd or even number. It can influence your accepting a double, for example.

Regardless of whether or not the Crawford Rule is in
use, when you get within 2 points of your goal, say 13 in
15-point match, try your utmost to win a double game.
To be within 1 point of your goal makes you vulnerable as
soon as all restrictions on the doubler are released. It is
not an enviable position, since in every game you play for
the rest of the match, you can lose, given backgammons, as
many as 6 points, whereas the most you can win is 1.
Therefore it is best to attempt to hurdle over 14 from 13 by
attempting to win the double game. Furthermore, if you
are at 13 and your opponent is at some lesser number, tend
to take doubles if you are in doubt, because if you win the
game you win the match.

Again, this is a paradox. To be at 14 is naturally better
than being at 13. Even so, at 14 you have problems which
would not otherwise exist. Your opponent controls the
doubler, and it is of little or no benefit to you. He may
double immediately at the beginning of every game *at no
risk*. It is true that he might also double immediately if you
were at 13, but he does so here at great risk, since you can
win not only the game but the match, which would not
have been true had he not doubled.

These details regarding unique or special uses of t
doubler are vital educational aids for the ambitious pla
er, and they are not difficult to learn or to remember.

Losing a gammon is the bugaboo of all backgamm
players; it is the prevailing danger against which playe
are warned from the very beginning. Yet in tournamer
there are situations where the loss of a double game
virtually no worse than losing a single game. Thou
most players fail to grasp this concept, it is a great adva
tage for those who do. But it only occurs in special situ
tions.

In a 15-point match, the score is 14−12 (or any less
even number) in favor of white, in Diagram 71. White h
a man on the bar and now rolls a 4-1. Ordinarily you a
taught to try to save a double game, but in this instance

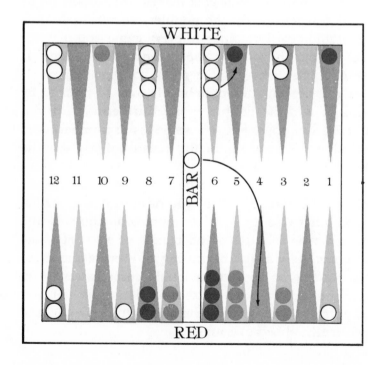

Diag
7

irrelevant, since you have virtually nothing to lose. If
our opponent gets to 14–14 in this particular game, he is
ot much better off than if he were at 14–13 with his dou-
ing privilege restored. The small advantage of the free
op is forfeited by white if he decides to go for the win
d thereby loses a gammon, but it is worth it to attempt to
inch the match on this game. The main danger to watch
r is the loss of a triple game. In this position, were white
come in on the 1 point and play the 4 elsewhere, he
ight even save a double game. But these should not be
s tactics. If he comes in on the 4 point, hits red's blot on
s 5 point and gets away with this bold play, it is his best
ance to win the game and the match even though he is a
stinct underdog to do so. However, it is most important
at he avoid losing a triple game, but oddly enough, by
ming in on the 4 point instead of the 1, he has mini-
ized this danger. Triple games usually occur when a
ayer holds his adversary's 1 point and remains there for a
ng time. In sum, our recommended move is a bold but
ecessary play.

A variation of this principle occurred in another tour-
ament match. The match was being played to 15 and the
ore was 14–8 in favor of red. In the position shown in
iagram 72, white, having waited intentionally, now dou-
ed. In both tournaments and money games, red would
nd to drop, but given the score—that is, 14 to any lesser
en number—red should take every time.

The subtle logic here is that since white is at 8, he
eeds four consecutive victories to win the match—ex-
uding double games and assuming that it is legal for him
double and that he does so in each successive game after
e opening roll. But if he were at 9 instead of at 8, he
ould need only three victories to win the match. There-
re, since being at 9 is virtually as good as being at 10,
hite should double, hoping to bluff red into dropping. In

over 90 percent of such cases the bluff would work.
white accomplishes this, he has, in effect, won a game
default and increased his chances of winning the mat
because he now needs only three victories instead of four

On the other hand, in this instance red should take tl
double, regardless of the hopelessness of his position
unless, of course, there were any danger of losing a gar
mon. Should red accept the double and lose, the score w
now be 14–10 in his favor, which is barely worse tha
14–9. The point being that the man who is behind is a
ways trying to get from even to odd, and this is what red
trying to obstruct. Since the comparative values of 9 an
10 are almost the same, red accepts what appears to be a
insane double (which in all money games he would dro

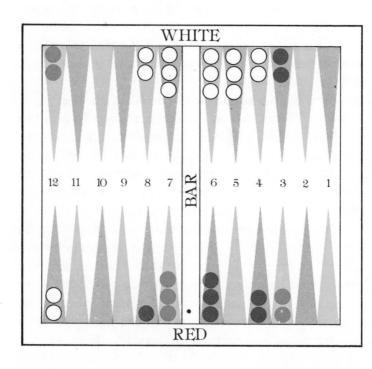

Dia
7

cause if he loses this game he has lost nothing extra,
d if he should win, he wins the match.

Any time you have a substantial lead on the score in a
urnament and have accepted a double, there is almost no
sition which will arise subsequently in which you
ould redouble. For example, in a recent tournament an
pert was playing an average player in a 23-point match.
d was ahead 18–11 (certainly a substantial lead) and
d accepted a double to 2 from white, the expert. The
sition then changed in red's favor and he redoubled to 4.
hite accepted, and a roll or two later, though still well
hind, he redoubled to 8. The reason for the redouble is
vious. If white loses at 4, he will be behind even more,
–11, and is virtually out of the match. Therefore this is
must game for him—hence the redouble. As luck would
ve it, disaster struck red and white won a gammon or 16
ints, winning the match 27–18. Red had no one to
ame but himself. He broke a cardinal rule by redoubling
the first place and deserved precisely what he got. If you
double in such circumstances, you are giving your oppo-
nt enormous leverage and have reserved none for your-
lf. Had red won the game at 2, he would have held a 20–
lead; even had he lost the 2, he would still have led 18–
. Thus, red in effect threw the game away.

In tournament play, *one* game can determine the out-
me of the match. This is more true of tournaments than
money games or chouettes. The game is a series of
l-or-nothing skirmishes, and unlike war, all victories are
mplete and absolute. The point to remember is that
thing in backgammon is irrelevant. There are no flights
fancy, no odds and ends. Everything is built upon some-
ing else—logic upon logic upon logic. And at the heart
it all is the doubler—the ruling element without which
ckgammon would be just another lottery. Unless the

beginner understands the doubler, he, like the gentlem
from Armenia, will never be more than an average comp
itor.

The Pip Count

The so-called pip count is an inexact method of det
mining which side is ahead, and by how much, after
contact between the sides has ceased—that is, when be
armies have maneuvered their forces beyond one anotl
and there will be no further contact by either side.

To determine your own and your opponent's pip cou
is simple but tedious arithmetic. Any men on your 1 po
count 1 point apiece, the men on your 2 point coun
points apiece and so on throughout the board. There ar
total of 24 points, so should you have any men on yc
opponent's 1 point, they would count 24 apiece. Obviou
there would still be contact were this the case, howev
and logically speaking the pip count would not be e
ployed in this instance.

At the beginning of the game, each player has a cou
of 167. When you understand how this figure is det
mined, you will be able to make an accurate count of bc
your position and your opponent's at any stage during t
game. Your two men in your opponent's inner board are
apiece, or 48. Your five men on his 12 point are 13 apie
or 65. The three men on your 8 point are 8 apiece, or :
and the five men on your 6 point are 6 apiece, or 30—ma
ing a total of 167.

Should you be considering doubling, the followi
formula is normally applied to ascertain the relative po
tions of both sides. If the pip count for both sides is o
100, you should be between 15 and 20 pips ahead to dc

le, but at least 20 ahead to redouble. (Remember that the
wer your pip count is, the farther you are ahead.) Con-
ersely, tend to take a double if you are less than 20 pips
ehind and perhaps drop if over 20. We say "perhaps,"
nce we naturally dislike dropping in these positions.
'here is no chance of a double game, and the game still
as a long way to go. If both sides are between 90 and 100
ips, you should be at least 13 pips ahead to double; be-
ween 80 and 90, 10 pips ahead; between 70 and 80, 7; and
etween 60 and 70, 5.

When both sides are under 50 pips, the basic fallacies
1 the pip count begin to become evident. We do not rec-
mmend using the pip count at all, but particularly when
1e count is under 50. The amount of time and effort it
akes to add this, that and these; to make the same compu-
ations for your opponent; and then to subtract one from
1e other in order to decide whether or not to double, ad-
les the brain and depletes energy that could be put to bet-
er use determining tactics and strategies in the ensuing
ame. Make no mistake, when you begin to take backgam-
1on seriously, stamina—both mental and physical—be-
omes a salient requirement, and the pip count is a partic-
larly exhausting and essentially useless form of mental
alisthenics. In baseball terms, it is a bit like requiring the
itcher to warm up between innings. As it is, the astute
ackgammon player is making enough continuous calcula-
ons without resorting to additional arithmetic.

The basic fallacy of the pip count can be shown in
1any ways. Consider the position shown in Diagram 73.
Vhite has two men on the 1 point, two on the 2 point and
wo on the 3 point, for a pip count of 12. Red has two men
n the 3 point and four men on the 1 point, a pip count
f 10. If it is white's roll, there can be no argument that
ed should refuse the double. But if it were red's roll—

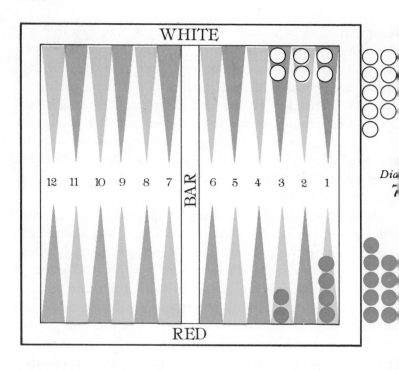

remember that he is 2 pips ahead—and he doubled, whi¹
would have a clear-cut take. If red rolled any 2 except do¹
ble 2's, white should even redouble. In other words, wit¹
only three rolls or less remaining in the game, white, wh¹
is *behind* in the pip count doubles and his opponent mu¹
drop. And in the same position, if the pip-count lead¹
doubled, his opponent would have to take. This exampl¹
also shows that when bearing off the even diversificatio¹
of your men in your inner board is infinitely more impo¹
tant than the pip count.

In Diagram 74, red has two men left on his 6 point,
pip count of 12, and white has three men on his 1 point,
pip count of 3. Red is 9 pips behind, it is his roll and h¹
has a mandatory double. So much for the pip count.

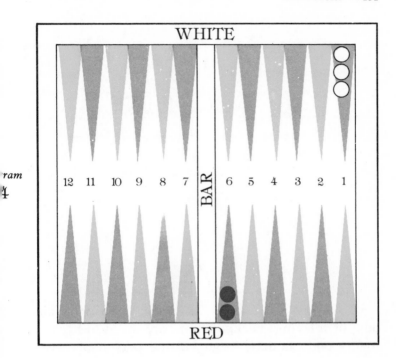

ram
4

If you have been playing backgammon for a long peri-
d, you should be able to determine your position and your
pponent's at a glance and know whether or not you are
ess than 3 to 1 to win. Even so, there are players who con-
nue to use the pip count despite the fact that it is little
ore than a long detour toward the same goal; it is remi-
iscent of the awkward counting movements beginners
mploy when moving their men about the board. Use it if
ou must, if it actually helps you, but if you learn to rec-
gnize the game's position at any given moment in the
atch, you will have accomplished a great deal more and
far less time.

◄8►

CHOUETTE

War is a constant state of reciprocal
action, the effects of which are mutual.

—Karl von Clausewitz

The three principal met
ods of playing backgammon are head-to-head, tourn
ments and chouette—that is, one person playing again
a field of two or more players. Because it is not a due
chouette in its broadest sense is the most civilized and s
cial form of the game, inspiring both competitiveness ar
camaraderie.

Chouette is organized in an order of strict rotatio
Any number of players may participate, but an ideal grou
is four or five. To begin a chouette, each player rolls a si
gle die. The one who rolls the highest number is called *t*
man in the box or simply *the box,* and he competes again
all the others. The man rolling the second highest numb
becomes *the captain* of the opposing side, and he will pla
and roll the dice. All others become the captain's partner
and though for the moment they cannot play, they ma
confer with the captain on all his moves and act as a kir
of general staff. But though they may advise, they are ult
mately bound by all the captain's decisions, except wh

fered a double; then, regardless of what the captain does, ey may accept or refuse as they see fit.

Throughout play, the rotation order is maintained. If e man in the box wins, he remains there, the defeated ptain goes to the bottom of the order and each player in rn becomes the new captain. If, however, the captain ins, he becomes the new holder of the box, displacing the an who has just lost, and who is now relegated to the ottom of the order on the opposing team.

In the scoring of chouette, the box competes against ich of the other players. If he is playing against, say, four pponents and wins a 1-point game, he is +4 and each of e others is −1. On the other hand, if the box loses, he is 4 and each of the other players is +1.

During a game the box may double and the captain ay decide to retire, but one or more of his advisers may cide to accept the double. If this occurs, the player clos- t to the top of the rotation who has accepted becomes the ptain and plays. If he wins, he becomes the man in the x and the other players rotate in the normal way. A rtner who decides not to accept a double is no longer the game and cannot advise the captain further, but by clining a double, he does not lose his place in the order play.

Because the man in the box is alone, it has been aimed that there is a small but definite percentage oper- ing against him. The reason put forward for this is that if makes a miscalculation, it will not be pointed out to m, whereas if the captain of the opposing side blunders, has two, three or even more advisers who can spot and rrect their captain's error before he picks up his dice. It assumed that because there are four minds at work on e same problem, there is less margin for error, and that erefore the percentages are in their favor. This is proba-

bly true, but the box has compensating advantages. B
cause he is playing by himself, he can make the moves
his choice without interference or argument and need n
ther explain nor defend his tactics to anyone. More impo
tantly, he is given the privilege of preempting any and a
deals among the other players. Concerning deals and se
tlements, he is the game's sole judge and adjudicator.

For instance, a controversy may arise as to whether
not to double the box. Let us assume that the captain
player A — and player B wish to double, but that C and
think it a poor idea. Further, let us assume that those pr
ferring to double offer to buy out the objectors by givi
them a point apiece for their respective games. An agre
ment is reached and the captain now doubles. The man
the box now has various options. He may agree to play a
four games or to drop them. Or he may preempt either
both of C and D's games; that is, according to the laws
chouette, he can give C 1 point and play three games, or
can give both C and D a point apiece and play the oth
two games. This rule is an enormous advantage to hi
since it gives him a greater scope should he wish to hedg

On the other hand, assume that the box doubles ever
body. Each contestant decides whether or not he will a
cept the double. Player A decides to refuse; player B, o
the other hand, decides it is a clear-cut take and not on
takes it himself, but offers to take player A's game as we
Again the man in the box has the right to veto the arrang
ment, insisting that player A drop to him and not to one
the other players.

Whenever any settlement is made among the oth
players, the box gets first acceptance or refusal, regardle
of the amount. He has all claims of prior right. Suppo
the bearing-off stage has been reached and a blot has be
left. This is a settlement situation (the intricacies of whi

will discuss in the next chapter). All kinds of demands
d offers are heard—not only among the partnership, but
tween the box and the partnership. Again, if any agree-
ents are reached between the other players, the box has
e right to intervene and take the settlement for himself.

Thus, on balance, despite the fact that the box is
one, we believe that the percentages are in his favor
ther than against him. The vital point to remember in
ouette is that the important games are those played in
e box. Whenever you are in the box, therefore, remember
at these are the decisive battles and that the degree of
ur gains and losses will be settled here.

Your golden opportunities will almost always occur in
e box, particularly when you can win two or three con-
cutive games. When this happens, there is a tendency for
ur adversaries to steam; having only the slightest of ad-
ntages, they will tend to double, hoping to pressure you
ematurely into surrender. Time after time in instances of
is kind, we have seen the box retire on the grounds that
has won enough, that he must not be greedy, that hav-
g won two or three games in a row, he should now con-
rve his new-found wealth. This is not only cowardly but
olish. At such moments the box is being offered what
nounts to an emotional double, and instead of dropping
should take. It is criminal to lose your nerve when you
e in a hot streak. When the opposing players, falling be-
nd and wrangling among themselves, offer neurotic
ubles, the box should accept them with the joy of a man
ho receives a gift he had not expected. Whenever the
emy is rash, it is a time to attack, not to preserve your
ins and retire.

Another point might be mentioned here. The concept
"greed" is sometimes greatly misunderstood. Backgam-
on essentially is a series of calculated risks. There is no

reason to be foolhardy, but don't retrench when you
going well. For instance, assume that you are 100 perce
certain to win a game if you play a move a certain way. *
alternative way makes you only a 7 to 1 favorite—but y
will win a double game if you get away with it. Which p
is correct? It's not even close; in a money game, play it t
second way every time. You're not being greedy by doi
so; you are simply playing the percentages and taking
calculated risk.

After the box has doubled in a chouette, a situati
may arise which is called a *drop-take*. In other words, ha
ing been doubled, two of the players may decide to acce
one double jointly and to drop the other, thereby minim
ing their potential loss. Thus, if the box is against tw
other players and they decide on a drop-take, the box w
automatically win 1 point, and with the doubler now at
will either win a total of 3 points or lose 1. The two pa
ners will either lose 3 points or win 1. This of course pr
supposes that there is no further doubling or gammon.

Often there are so many players in a chouette that t
box will take a partner in order to lessen his risk. Th
usually happens when six or more players are in the gam
therefore, instead of being one against five, say, it will nc
be two against four. The box may select any member of t
opposing team as his partner, providing the player is agre
able, and this usually leads to the best player in t
chouette being chosen constantly. A superior method is
force the box, should he wish a partner, to select the play
he has just defeated. There is a pervasive logic in th
method; it eliminates any favoritism. When the box c
select anyone to partner him, it may be awkward for t
chosen player. This is especially true if the nominee
constantly picked. He is not obligated to comply, but it
insulting to refuse. If a fair rotation system is devise

however, none of these unpleasant situations arise.

Depending on whether or not you are a member of the general partnership or on your own in the box, the strategies of your game should fluctuate. As a partner, you should accede to the majority opinion. This should be done even when you feel the wrong percentage play is being made. Given the fickle make-up of the game, the wrong move may miraculously be right; secondly, everyone is playing for pleasure as well as money, and by not voicing your discontent you contribute to the feeling of good will at the table. More importantly, in any game in which you are not in the box, you are playing for only 25 percent of the stake if there are, say, five players. In addition, if all of the captain's advisers object to his proposed move, he should comply with the majority opinion, though if he cared to, he could insist on his own way. These are the manners of backgammon, the game's civilities.

As we have said, you play your most crucial games in chouette when you are in the box. This may seem obvious, but we have seen and continue to witness among the group opposing the box violent arguments, growing occasionally so heated that a player will actually quit and walk away in anger. Since such a player usually stands to lose only a third or a quarter of the total stake, this is absurd behavior; yet wherever chouette is played these altercations occur. Resolve never to indulge in such foolishness; even if a technical error is made now and then, relax and let the captain play it his way. In the long run, you'll save time and avoid petty and unnecessary disputes.

In Europe there is a colorful custom called *giving for games*. Any backgammon player in or out of the chouette can, should he like either side, utter the words "Giving for games." This means that he will give whatever the amount of the doubler is at the moment to any and all participants

for their respective games. He does this because he b
lieves a double is in order, and of course he immediate
doubles. The participants must either go along with t
double or give over their games to the newcomer. It is
ironclad rule. If it is the box that is being doubled, he m
preempt any or all the games, giving the necessary poir
to as many of his opponents as he wishes. Or he may a
cept the double outright for all the games.

There is a great risk for anyone who makes the offer
"giving for games." He immediately gives the number
points on the doubler to each player and proceeds to pl
for twice that number. Thus, if he loses (assuming no
double or double game), he loses 3 units, whereas his ma
imum profit is only 1. This applies to all the games he h
bought, so he must be very sure of the position when off
ing the proposition.

Anyone already playing in the chouette may also s
"giving for games" and take over. The only time the tact
is not permitted is when one side is obviously playing for
gammon.

"Giving for games" is a colorful addition, especial
if a few wild early-doublers are loose in the vicinity. Som
one will walk in, notice that because there are so ma
players he will not be able to play for a long time if l
starts at the bottom of the rotation, and therefore a
nounces, "Giving for games." If he is fortunate, he w
vault immediately into the box. There is more fun tha
science in this European innovation, and since no one
ever forced to make this highly speculative offer, it h
become one of backgammon's more amusing eccentricite

Contrary to your style of play as a member of the par
nership, playing alone in the box should not affect yo
tactics in any way. You should play against four or fi
opponents as boldly as against one, and not flinch simp

cause the stakes are higher. If you are doubled, and it is
double you would normally take, you should take it here.
 take is a take; nothing but the position of the game
ould influence your decision. If the sum involved dis-
rbs you, your abilities are being affected adversely.

The simplest method of determining just what stakes
u should play for in chouette is to multiply the stake by
e number of players in the game excluding yourself. For
ample, if the stake is $1 a point and there are four people
 the game, you must ask yourself whether you are com-
rtable playing for $4 a point and whether you will be able
 take a double to $8 with equanimity. If you can, play; if
t, find another game.

Some years ago in London, a striking example of the
akes you should not play for occurred in a chouette. A
an called Gravita was playing against eight other men,
ost of whom were excellent players. Gravita had been
sing steadily for years, but he enjoyed the game and al-
ays paid his debts. On this particular evening the stakes
ere set at £20 (about $50) a point. Toward the end of the
ening, Gravita was somewhat ahead, but the game at
nd was going against him. The doubler had been turned
ck and forth to 64, and in mid-game the partnership,
nsing an advantage, redoubled Gravita to 128.

Gravita hesitated, then laughed and said, "Well, gen-
men, I can't afford to pay if I drop, so I'll take it." (Had
 dropped, his loss would have been $25,576.) Everyone
iled; Gravita was known for his little jokes. But when
e game ended, Gravita found that he had lost a double
me, or $102,304. He stood up from the table, walked
t of the room, and to this day, no one has ever seen
ravita again. As a result, whenever anyone in London
kes a bad double, it is known as a "Gravita Take."

◄9►

SETTLEMENTS

It is from the character of our adversary's
position that we can draw conclusions as
to his designs and will, therefore,
act accordingly.

— *Karl von Clausewitz*

Settlements are an impo[r]
tant strategy in all money games, and though they are us[ed]
in European tournaments, they are not as yet allowed in t[he]
United States. A settlement is a compromise negotia[ted]
between the opposing sides, wherein one army agrees [to]
give up a portion of the disputed stake in return for [an]
immediate end to the hostilities. It is a complicated form [of]
bargaining in which one faction attempts to buy off t[he]
other by saying, in effect, "Surrender this much now [or]
ultimately I may take it all." Settlements are the gam[e of]
politics.

Given the esoteric mathematical hagglings such neg[o]
tiations involve, many players of backgammon have ch[o]
sen the simplest course: they never settle. One man of o[ur]
acquaintance plays regularly in a running chouette. He [is]
a better than average player but knows nothing about t[his]
facet of the game and therefore has adopted the tactic [of]
refusing all settlements, regardless of how attractive th[ey]
may seem. By refusing settlements he reasons that he w[ill]

least break even. It is sound strategy, since he is incapa-
~~e~~ of determining how much he should give or take in
~~sp~~ecific situations.

But the art of settlements is not as difficult as it may at
~~fir~~st appear, and since these proposals to compromise usu-
~~all~~y occur at crucial moments in the game, a rudimentary
~~un~~derstanding of how they work can be beneficial. Settle-
~~m~~ents may crop up in the middle of the game, but normal-
~~ly~~ they are made toward the end, when the game suddenly
~~ta~~kes, or seems about to take, an unexpected turn from cer-
~~ta~~in victory to defeat, or from defeat to possible victory.
~~D~~uring these crucial moments, when, for example, the
~~pl~~ayer in the stronger position sees that his superiority
~~m~~ay be undermined, or the player in the weaker position
~~ca~~n turn the game around by rolling one specific number,
~~pl~~ayers may attempt to reach an immediate compromise
~~ra~~ther than risk the whole stake. If a player can determine
~~th~~e precise odds against his winning or losing, in situa-
~~tio~~ns of this kind it is not difficult to compute what per-
~~ce~~ntage of the stake he should either take or give.

In all settlements there is a basic formula to use. Take
~~th~~e recurring position in which red is bearing off and
~~le~~aves a blot which if hit will give white the game. It is a
~~25~~ to 11 shot in favor of red. The doubler is at 32. Since
~~w~~hite is the underdog, how much should white give? On
~~an~~ average of 36 games, given the odds, red will win 25
~~an~~d lose 11, for a net gain of 14. If you multiply 14 (his net
~~ga~~in) by 32 (the stake), you get a figure of 448. Dividing
~~th~~is figure by 36 (the number of games played), you get an
~~ex~~act settlement of 12.44. Since 12 is the nearest whole
~~nu~~mber, 12 is the correct settlement that white should give
~~to~~ red. You will note that the underdog gets a tiny edge
~~he~~re, since he should give 12.44, but this kind of fraction
~~is~~ generally overlooked.

But just because you know the fair settlement is 12 no way commits you to negotiate that figure. Though helps if you at least know what the fair figure is, it is n considered unethical to ask for more if you are red, or offer less if you are white. Both sides are bargainin Sometimes unfair settlements are intentionally offere since the less skillful player is either ignorant or confus by settlements, he may accept a lesser amount or surrend a greater amount than the correct figure.

There have even been cases in which the less skillf settler, having been offered *more* than he deserved, h demanded even more than that. In a money game played few years ago, a position arose in which red had four m remaining on his 1 point and white had two. This positi is illustrated in Diagram 75. Red needed any double in der to win the game. The doubler was at 64 on red's side a white offered a settlement. What would the correct offer b

Thirty shots lose for red and six (the six doubles) w so he was exactly a 5 to 1 underdog. Again, using the f mula — in 36 games, white will win 30 and lose 6 for a gain of 24. As before, multiply 24 by 64 (the stake), whi is 1,536. Divide by 36 (the number of games played) a we get $42\frac{2}{3}$, or, to the nearest whole number, 43. B this was the last game, and for other reasons white was prepared to court disaster. Thus, in a burst of generosit he offered to take only 32, 11 points less than he was tec nically entitled to.

Red was behind and steaming. He considered the pr posal, looked up and said, "You want *32?* I'm not givi you anything. As a matter of fact, I'm going to double y to 128." Red was amazed, but he shrugged and accept the double. White then rolled double 4's to win the gam and red, for the hundredth time, wondered why he had ev become involved in this cruelest game.

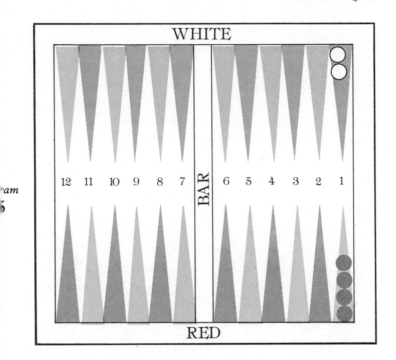

WHITE

12 11 10 9 8 7 BAR 6 5 4 3 2 1

RED

To date, settlements are not permitted in American tournaments, which is unfortunate, for they are a definite part of the game. Should beginners find them difficult, they have only to refuse. In Europe, however, they are allowed and contribute greatly to the game. Recently, in an important London tournament, red, an experienced and wily player, was pitted against a comparative beginner. They were playing a 15-point match with no Crawford rule, and white was ahead 13–12. The doubler was at 2 on white's side, and the match had progressed to a critical position in a critical game (see Diagram 76). At this juncture, red, whose turn it was, said, "I'll take 1 point." The offer looked and seemed reasonably fair, since white had to roll a double to win. But white was uncertain, and after thinking about it declined the settlement.

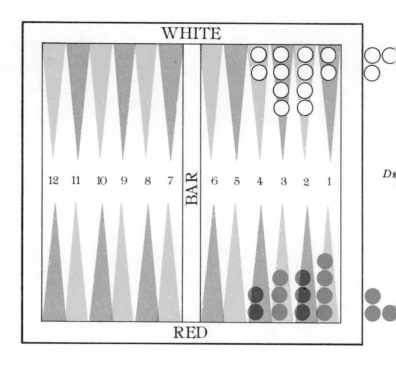

The game continued and after four rolls by red a
three by white, neither red nor white having rolled a do
ble (see Diagram 77), red halted play before white's r
and again made the same offer. "Perhaps I'm foolish,"
said, "since it's three rolls later and I'm in much bet
shape than before. I'm probably getting the worst of it, b
I'll still take 1 point." On this occasion white, seeing th
red would be off in two rolls and that he still needed a do
ble to win, relented; he agreed to the offer of the point a
the score became 13 – 13.

Before reading on, try to determine which of the tv
got the better of the deal. Was it unfair or fair? It is, in fa
probably the most outlandish swindle imaginable. B
why?

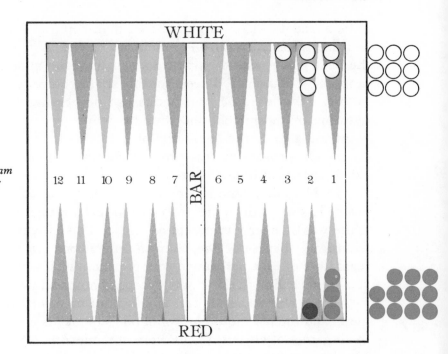

gram 77

Consider the situation. There is no Crawford Rule, so here are no restrictions on the doubler. They are playing to 5 and white is ahead 13–12. If the doubler had been on ed's side in any money game in this position, it would be clear-cut drop. Also in any money game, an offer to take by red should be promptly accepted by white. But in this pecial instance, white has virtually nothing to gain and everything to lose by conceding a point. What he has failed o comprehend is that this is the game that can win the natch. Had white played out the game and lost, the score vould have been 14–13 against him. This is no worse han being 13–13, which the score became when the offer vas accepted. Behind 14–13, white will certainly double on the first roll of the next game. (You will remember that to be ahead 14–13 is slightly better than being at 13–13 because when your opponent doubles on the first roll of the next game, which he will do, you have the choice of dropping if you wish.) Except for this slight compensation, however, the loss of 1 or 2 points had no bearing on the outcome of the match, and thus for white to concede a point and give up the possibility of rolling a double to win the match was lunacy. It is hard to conceive of a more lopsided settlement in favor of red.

Incidentally, there was nothing unethical in red's proposal. It was little more than a political gesture which white was at liberty to accept or refuse. This is what bargaining is all about. The point to remember here is that regardless of how persuasive your opponent is, if you *know* you are receiving the best of it, accept; if not, decline.

To be able to settle well is a form of money management, and the judicious control of one's money is essential in all games of chance. Oddly, correct money management often goes against the odds—and rightly so. For instance, assume that you have $10,000 to your name and no other assets of any kind. You are approached by a man with $20,000 who requires an additional $10,000. He offers to bet his money against yours on the flip of a coin. It is an even-money bet. Would you accept? It is the sort of situation bookmakers and professional gamblers dream about, for you are getting 2 to 1 on an even-money bet. But though the bet adheres to the normally excellent axiom which states that when you have the best of a proposition, bet all you can, it would be folly to accept the challenge. There is another axiom which states that when you are down to your case money, never bet it all on one roll, regardless of the odds you get. Today is important in the world of chance, but not when it eliminates tomorrow.

This is an example of wise money management ignor-

g the odds. This sound principle is applied particularly
places like Las Vegas, where casinos not only have the
est of the odds, but limit the size of your stake as well. It
a sensible practice, since it would be possible for some-
ne on a streak actually to break the house. The limit
hich the casinos impose on their clientele is an essential
rm of money management.

In backgammon the same principle should be applied.
e wary of games that become so high and wild that in
der to manage your money properly you must take the
orst of the odds. Suppose, for example, that you are in a
e-handed chouette at $5 a point, a stake somewhat high-
than you usually play for, and that the doubler has
mehow been turned and turned to 64. You are in the box
d are feeling distinctly uncomfortable. While bearing
f, you leave a blot. Your opponents have a single shot; it
25 to 11 against their hitting you, but if they do, they
in the game. At this point they offer you a settlement.
he correct settlement in this example is 25, but you
ould take much less; in fact, you would take almost any-
ing you could get. By allowing this kind of situation to
evelop, you have squandered valuable equity. Avoid these
edicaments and play only in games where settling de-
nds exclusively on the position and not on the financial
atastrophe that would occur should your opponents ob-
in the right roll.

In backgammon there are certain "insurance" situa-
ons in which players will intentionally take the worst of
e odds. This is most frequent in the final matches of a
urnament when one player reaches a position whose
ds can be calculated exactly.

An example of this occurred in the finals of a recent
hampionship match. Each player had 16 points in a 17-
oint match, and victory would be decided on the final roll

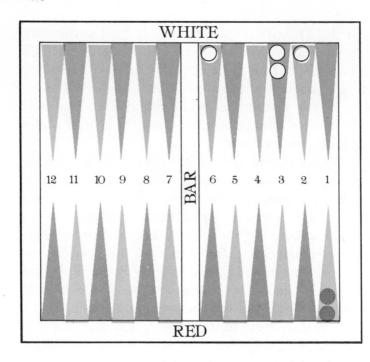

WHITE

12 11 10 9 8 7 | BAR | 6 5 4 3 2 1

RED

Diag
7

of the final game. In that final position (see Diagram 7?
red, an Englishman, had two men left on his 1 poin
White, an excellent player from the Far East, had four me
left, one of them on his 6 point. It was white's roll, and s
he needed double 6's to win the first prize of $6,500. *A*
this point, red stopped the game in order to take insuranc
against the possibility of white rolling double 6's—th
odds of which, you will recall, are 35 to 1 against.

Red extracted a $100 bill from his pocket, turned *t*
the crowd of spectators and asked what odds he could ge
One spectator said he would give red 30 to 1 against th
double 6's, and red agreed. Another offered red 31 to
against for a further outlay of $100, and again red agree
Of course red knew he was getting the worst of the odd

ıt in this case it was worth it as insurance against the
ɔtential disaster of double 6's.

It was white's roll, and he promptly threw double 6's
win the match. By losing, red collected not only the
?,500 second prize, but also a total of $6,100 from the two
ɔectators — $2,100 more than he would have received had
ɛ won the tournament. As the crowd surged round the
ble congratulating the players, a woman turned to anoth-
 spectator and asked, "Aren't the true odds against dou-
e 6's 35 to 1?" "No," the man said, "not when a China-
ɩan's rolling."

◄10►
END·GAME TACTICS

The art of war is largely an art of
manoeuvre. The effectiveness of a fighting
unit depends on the coordination
of its parts.

—*Karl von Clausewitz*

To have the ability to im
provise, to deviate when necessary from the norm, is th
hallmark of the best backgammon players. Too man
others, once they have learned the fundamentals and a
quired a certain low panache, play the game for the rest
their lives as though it were parcheesi. This is particular
true toward the end of the game during that last sw
sprint into the inner board. We have seen players movin
their men as mechanically as a Monopoly counter. Yet th
strategies employed at this stage are among the most su
tle and important in backgammon.

A case in point is the artful deployment of 1's. In Di
gram 79, red rolls double 1's. Red's position is bad, but n
hopeless. He is attempting to preserve his board and r
quires delay. Paradoxically, the way to accomplish this
to rush all four men on his bar into his inner board. Th
apparently eccentric play prevents red from being forced
move 6's. If any of these four men remained on the ba
it would have to be played down to the 1 point if a 6 we
rolled, and red does not want these men out of play. Thu

am

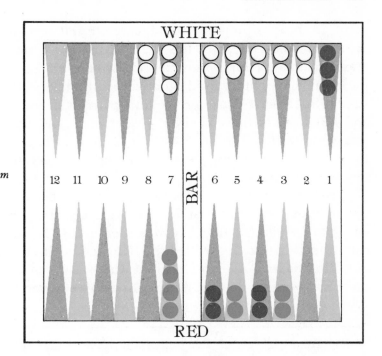

cause delay, red rushes his men forward. A contradic-
on in terms, but correct and logical.

In Diagram 80, very different tactics are required. The
tuation looks similar but is almost completely opposite.
ed is well ahead in a running game, though he has left
hind a rear guard of two men on white's bar point. Un-
ss cunning delaying tactics are employed, almost certain-
one of these men, and perhaps both of them, will be cap-
red. In this position, red again rolls double 1's. He must
w protect himself from being forced to play a 6 from
hite's bar point. Since he is far ahead in a race, he is in
ttle hurry to put the men in from his bar point. More
portantly, he can use them to play 6's and thereby pro-
ct the stragglers on white's bar point. The correct play is
move one man from his 6 point down to make his 2

point. In this position red should leave himself as many ε
as he can, the reverse of the tactic of the preceding di
gram. In this example most players would tend to ma
the right move, but would ignore it in the preceding i
stance. Such plays illustrate the fluid patterns of the gam
and variations of these positions occur again and again
late-game tactics. If you learn to apply these concepts
these specific instances, they will strengthen every depaι
ment of your game.

An extreme example of a paradoxical play occurred
a tournament in Switzerland a few years ago. In a mate
going to 15 points, the score was even at 13–13. In tl
penultimate game, red rolled a 5-4 in the position illu
trated in Diagram 81. No Crawford Rule was in effect ar
there had been no double. After considerable deliberatio

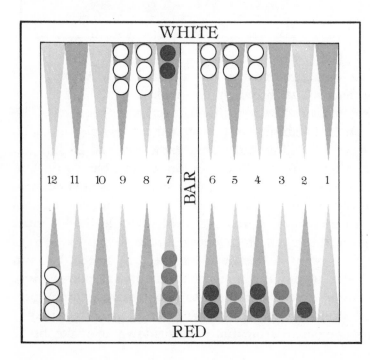

Di

ε

d moved one man from his 9 point to his 5 point, and
other from his 6 point to make his 1 point. Red could, of
urse, have moved his man on white's 5 point all the way
his own 11 point, thereby escaping white — as white was
ick to point out to red when the game had ended. But
e reasoning in this instance was more involved. To run
d win a single point gave red virtually no advantage ex-
pt the dubious one of dropping in the next game when
ite doubled, as he was bound to do after the opening
l. By staying and holding his ground, red risked losing
e game, but it also gave him a slight chance of winning a
uble game and the match; therefore he thought it worth
e risk. For example, if white had thrown a 3-1 or a 5-3
the next roll, he would have had to give red a 7 shot,
th perhaps worse still to come. (Of course, white could

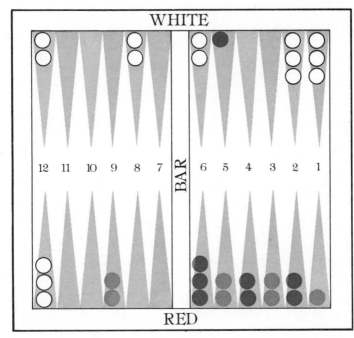

*ram

1

play two men down from the 6 point with the 5-3, but t[
would leave him more vulnerable than ever for the rest
the game.) It is imaginative thought of this kind that li
the level of the game and is yet another example of sou
improvisation.

In Diagram 82, red has brought in all his men exc
one, which remains on white's 9 point, and white has t
men on red's 4 point. Red has a 1 to play and has the c
tion of moving it up one point to white's 10 point. Ordin
ily the farther a man is from his adversary, the more di
cult he is to hit; thus, advancing by one point would a
pear to give white a slightly improved chance of hitti
him. But a little thought will show that leaving the man
the 9 point makes him vulnerable to double 6's, double
and double 3's, whereas if he moves to the 10 point, he

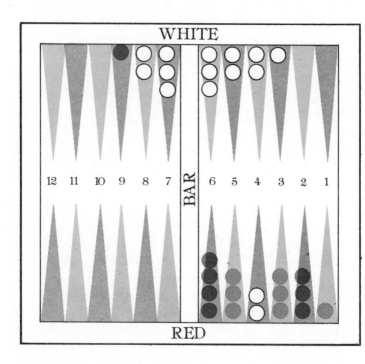

Dic

8

lnerable only to a 6-5. So it is correct to move one pip
)ser.

Examples of this kind may seem minuscule, but if you
sh to improve your game, such moves are vital. Nor
)uld such computations deter you. No more than a
ade-school knowledge of arithmetic is necessary; given
at, you will have acquired a definite edge over the player
10 tends to scoff at such details.

Another tactic, referred to previously, often escaping
e beginner's attention, is hitting *too many* of your oppo-
:nt's men. Assume that red has a closed board and one of
1ite's men on the bar. If red is still coming around the
»ard and if white has left several blots, red should pick up
1ly enough of them to assure the double game. (Ordinar-
' four men are sufficient.) Superficially, it would seem safe
iough to hit as many of his men as you please. But if you
:ked up eight men, for example, and then began bearing
f, it is quite possible that you would leave a blot. Had
hite had only four men on the bar, he would probably have
»me in by the time you had only, say, your lower three
»ints left, but with eight, there is a good chance of his re-
aining out until you are forced to leave a blot. Hit only as
any men as you need, no more. Don't vacuum the whole
ea; your greed could cost you the game.

In Diagram 83, white has rolled a 5-4. You will re-
:ember the rule that if you must leave a blot, you should
ove your men in such a way as to give your opponent the
ast number of shots. In this instance, however, the wiser
urse is to contradict the "percentage play." The play giv-
g red the least number of shots is to move one man from
e 6 point to the 1 point and the other from the 5 point to
e 1 point, leaving red a 1 to hit; or to move two men from
e 6 point, leaving red a direct 2. Each play leaves the
ast number of shots, but both are unconscionable, since

they destroy white's board and in all probability he will
worse off on his next roll. It is better, therefore, to se
an alternate way of playing the 5-4 even though it is le
safe. Many players would bring a 5 down from red's
point to their 8 point and play the 4 from white's 6 point
white's 2 point, leaving themselves vulnerable to a 1 and
some vague indirect shot (in this case, a 9). But this t
would be incorrect. Instead, white should bring both m
from the 12 point, one to the 8 point and the other to the
point, where he will be exposed to a direct 5 and a 3
This play might appear to be less safe, but it is much le
dangerous. To give these two extra shots is much sa
than giving the 1 and the 9. In the latter, the total numb
of shots that will hit is 16, whereas in the recommend

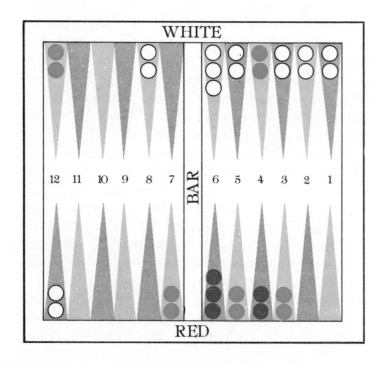

Dia

8

ay the number of shots that will hit is only 13. An addi-
nal advantage to this play is that it is easier to transport
ur blot to safety on the next roll. Again this is an exam-
e of a simple mathematical decision which happens in
ckgammon constantly.

In Diagram 84, white has been forced into what seems
be a frightening decision. White has a 1 to play and red
s a closed board. Most players become petrified at the
ght of an opponent's closed board and would tend to play
e 1 safely behind red's blot. But forget the danger for a
oment and examine the logic. If white decides not to hit,
d is certainly a favorite to win this game, since he is well
ead in a race. But if white hits, red has suddenly become
25 to 11 underdog, since he must roll a direct 5 to win

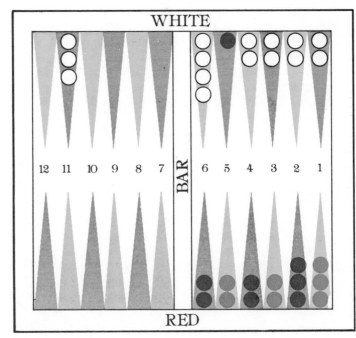

ram
4

the game. Thus, white must hit. There is more comm
sense than courage in this play. The only danger to co
sider is that white could lose a double game, but it is
mote and should not be taken seriously.

Diagram 85 is another example of what passes
bold decisive play. White is on the bar and rolls a 3
Many players would enter red's board on the 1 point a
use the 3 to save the man on their 9 or 7 point by bringi
it in to their inner board. But the move accomplishes no
ing and still leaves white dangerously exposed. The co
rect play is to enter red's board on the 3 point and to
the blot on white's 5 point by moving one man fro
white's 6 point to his 5 point, leaving two blots in
board. Once again, there is nothing particularly bold

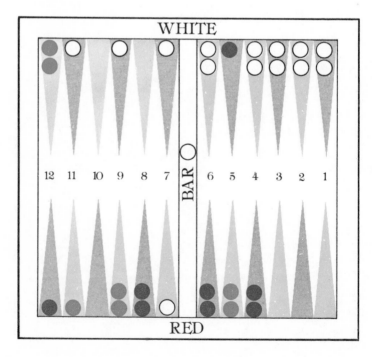

Di
8

is play; indeed, not to make it is certain suicide. When
nite can reduce his chances of being an almost certain
ser to being only a 5 to 4 underdog, he is not being bold.
ut due to the unnaturalness of this tactic, most players
ould not consider it. However, the play puts red on the
r, and if he does not throw a 5 or a 6 on his next roll,
nite will have strong double-game possibilities. If red
re not hit, he would have complete freedom of move-
ent to assault white's numerous blots and would almost
rtainly win a double game himself.

But assume that white enters and hits red. Should red
w double? In a money game, he should double every
ne. Under certain tournament conditions, depending to
me degree upon the relative abilities of the two players,
should not. Of course there are always special circum-
ances. If red is the weaker player, he should double even
ough he is on the bar, because he is trying to use the
ce to counteract his opponent's greater ability. But if he
the stronger player, he should not double, since he pre-
rs to have his technique hold sway, rather than the luck
ctor. To repeat: such decisions are always influenced by
e strengths and weaknesses of your adversary.

Often in late-game positions, it is the rolling of small
umbers that elicits the most subtle variations of play. In
e next three examples, the strategic movement of a 2-1
comes a crucial factor in the success or failure of red's
me. In Diagram 86, white has borne off 13 of his men,
d in this position red rolls a 2-1. In this instance there
only one correct play. Whenever your opponent has 13
en off, you must force him to break any point in order to
t both of his men on the bar. If he has your 1 point and
ou have established a prime, break the prime so that he
as to play a 6 if he rolls it. Red should move one man
om his bar point onto his 5 point and the other from

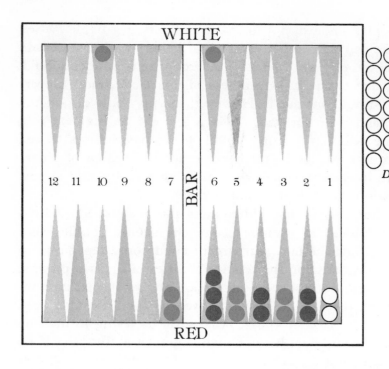

white's 10 point to the 11 point. Of course, double 6's m
win the game for white, but they would win the ga
anyway if red waited to break his bar point until all l
other men were in his inner board. Further, by leaving o
man on his bar point, red increases his chances of w
ning, since he will come in again in white's board if wh
throws a 6. The chief principle at work here is that
risks are worthwhile in order to separate white's two me

Again, in Diagram 87, white has borne off 13 men a
established a point in red's board. Red now rolls a 2
The principle is the same as in the previous diagram; r
must force white to break his anchor. The correct play
to move one man from white's 4 point up ·to his 6 po
and to move the 1 from red's 5 point to red's 4 point, le

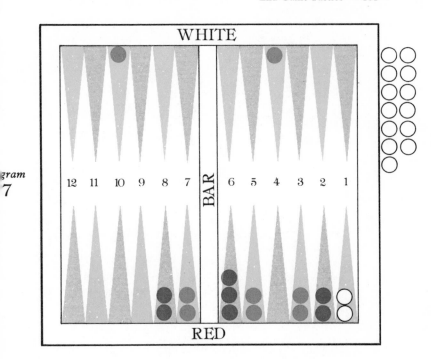

ing two blots in his inner board. This play gives white 3's
and 4's to move, and red hopes that white will be able to
hit one of his men. The oddity of this play should not deter
the beginner. It is logical and the strongest threat to
white's position. It also shows that red has devoted some
thought to his game and is alert to the potentialities of all
rolls.

In Diagram 88, white has borne off 12 of his men and
has established a forward point in red's board. Red now
rolls a 2-1. In this instance red appears to have several options, but again there is only one logical move. Red could
hit the blot on white's 4 point, but should not do so, since
his object is to break white's anchor. Almost any number
will cause white to do so, whereas if red hits, white will

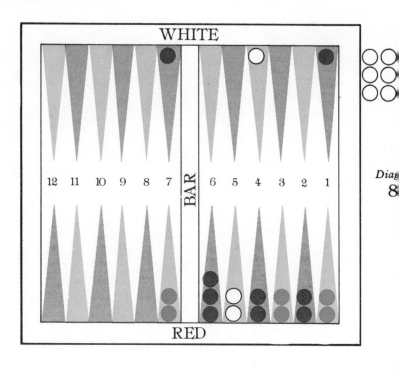

have to wait for 5's in order to re-enter — which will be
his advantage. Here the logical play is not to hit, forcir
white to run. Once that happens, red is in an excellent p
sition to capture all of white's three remaining men. Whe
this is accomplished, he may double and white shou
drop. Red's best play is to move the man on white's bar
his 10 point.

In conclusion, there are many late-game positior
involving the tactical deployment of two separate men
especially when you have borne the rest of your men c
the board. In positions of this kind, beginners seem parti
ularly confused and tend to push their remaining me
toward the 1 point with gloom and resignation. For exar
ple, in Diagram 89, red has two men left in his inner boar

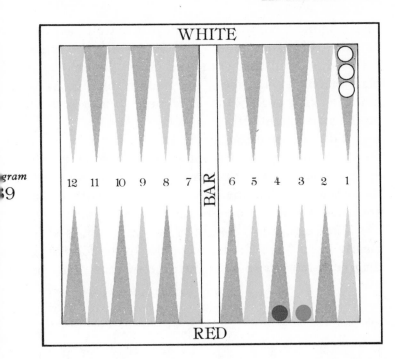

gram
9

n different points, having borne off the rest of them.
White has three men left on his 1 point. Red has a 1 to
play. In this situation a dilemma almost always arises as to
where to move the 1 in order to have the best chance of
taking both men off on the subsequent roll.

A general rule: with two men left, it is never wise to
double up—that is, to place both men on the same point. It
is usually better to move the front man forward. In the position shown, red is a 19 to 17 underdog to take both men
off on the next roll. The 1 is crucial here. To move from
the 4 point to the 3 point is irrelevant, since the same
number of shots will get both men off next time. Red
might just as well have left the man on the 4 point. (This
applies to any two men doubled up on the odd points—for

instance, the 5 point. You might just as well have one ma[n] on the 5 point and the other on the 6 point; the same num[-]ber of shots will bear both men off on the next roll.) Th[e] play, therefore, is to move the man on the 3 point to the [5] point, making red a 23 to 13 favorite to take both men o[ff] on the subsequent roll.

With two men remaining in your inner board, alway[s] tend to go toward the 1 point with the front man. The on[ly] exception to this is if you have one man on the 6 point an[d] the other on either the 2 or 3 points. In both these case[s] you should always move the man off the 6 point.

The paradoxical nature of backgammon is seen mo[re] clearly here. Take 7's, for example. In the following thr[ee] diagrams, red has in each instance two men left, and it [...]

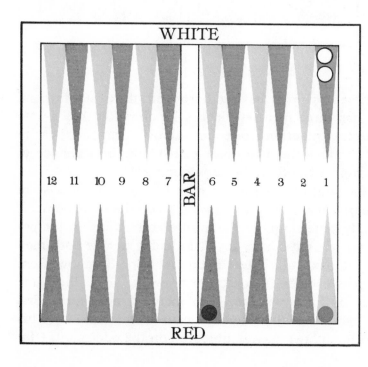

Diag[ram]
9[...]

is roll. In Diagram 90, he has one man on his 6 point and the other on his 1 point; in Diagram 91, he has one on his point and the other on his 2 point; in Diagram 92, he has ne on his 4 point and the other on his 3 point.

In Diagram 90, red is a 21 to 15 underdog to take both men off in one roll. But if the back man is one pip farther forward, and the front man one pip less advanced, as in Diagram 91, red becomes a 19 to 17 favorite to bear both men off. Yet if they are still closer together, as in Diagram 92, red becomes a 19 to 17 underdog. If one were to employ the pip count in each case, a total roll of 7 would get both of red's men off, and yet the odds of bearing them both off vary considerably. This is just one more indication of the pip count's inherent fallacies.

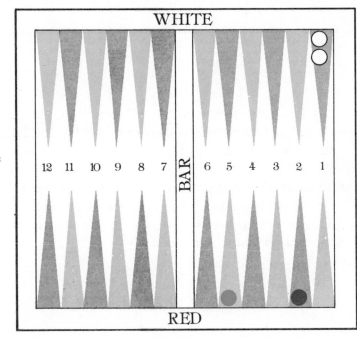

ram
1

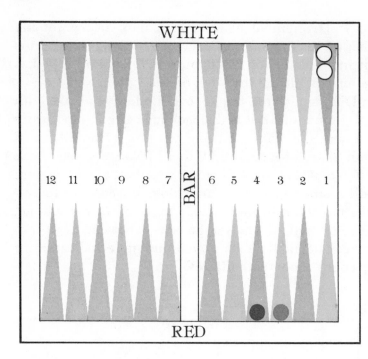

Dia
g

As has been demonstrated, all late-game play involv‹
astute tactical ability and a talent for making the right pe
centage play. In these final stages of the game, when o‹
combatant often has his back to the wall, there is no roo‹
for guesswork, and if you follow percentages and adhere
the inherent logic of the game, you will rarely have ‹
guess. Let your opponent guess. To guess in an either-‹
position is to make a mistake exactly 50 percent of t‹
time.

◄11►

THE PSYCHOLOGY OF THE GAME

All war supposes human weakness and
against that it is directed.

—Karl von Clausewitz

There are many reasons for
he tremendous resurgence of backgammon, but one aspect of the game in particular makes it unique. There is
no other game involving skill in which the beginner after
a short time reaches a level from which he has a definite
chance to beat anyone else, no matter how good his opponent. This is a built-in hazard for the experienced player,
a great boon for the newcomer and adds excitement for
kibitzers and participants alike.

The rules of the game are simple, their execution an
art; this is backgammon's pervasive principle. However, it
is the game's apparent simplicity that is its greatest attraction. Almost anyone can learn 60 percent of the moves in a
week, and we know of no one who did not believe that he
actually understood the game in a few days. But backgammon is so subtle that it may be impossible to learn *all*
there is to know about it. One of the world's leading players, who has played for thirty years, admits that he probably understands only 90 percent of the game. As you must

know by now, backgammon is more complex than it fi
appears to be.

Because of the subtle skills involved (most avera
players believe those who are better than themselves a
lucky), and because most players tend to rationalize t
dice, blaming their misfortunes on "bad luck," it is di
cult not only to recognize your mistakes, but to evalua
your abilities. The game is usually played for money, a
self-deception can be expensive. Given the luck, the se
deception, and the fact that there is no other game
which a player can so often make the wrong move and w
as a direct result of it, backgammon has become for ma
of its devotees an exquisite siren song, a honeyed land
hope and double 6's. It is for these reasons that we ha
called backgammon the cruelest game.

Like some concealed and irreplaceable mechanis
cruelty *is* built into the game. For example, it is repl
with paradox. Once the dice have been thrown, a bat
begins, and each succeeding roll will alter the position, t
tactics and the strategies. Certain basic theories, all sour
may have to be violated at any time. It is this elusive pri
ciple that is probably the most difficult to comprehend
and the most destructive when it is not brought into pla
The beginner will learn the fundamental rules — and w
then be told that he must contradict them. Though ma
players acquire other more mechanical skills, they nev
completely grasp this. But it is this flair for improvisati
which separates the average player from the expert. A go
player is one who plays his bad rolls well. A chronic los
loses because he is unable to play his difficult rolls to l
best advantage. Anyone knows how to bear off four m
when he has rolled double 6's.

All too often the wrong computation, the wrong de
sion, and hence the incorrect move will win. This is t

st unkindest cut of all. But it happens so often that
ayers who have won as a direct result of it attribute their
ccess to skill and believe the game requires no further
ıdy. Backgammon is glutted with such people. If one
empts to explain certain percentages to them, they are
erely insulted. When they lose in money games or tour-
ments, they will later confide to intimates that their
ponent was unbelievably lucky and their own dice unbe-
:vably bad.

In this aspect, no other game can be compared to
ckgammon. For example, if you challenged Bobby
scher at chess, and for some reason he accepted, you
ould not win a single game. In bridge, an inferior player
ll seldom win a tournament, and in poker the best player
ll almost always win.

Except for chess, there is an element of luck in the
ove games. In backgammon, however, the luck factor is
minant. Though many of the percentages in backgam-
on are calculable, the ratio between luck and skill re-
ains obscure and has probably been discussed for as long
the game has existed. Because it is not as logical as
ess or as scientifically exact as checkers (a game so re-
ictively formal that if two experts play, the one who
oves first always wins), it is often dismissed by the un-
owing as just one more game of chance performed by
mblers who might just as well be flipping coins.

Although the ratio of skill to luck is impossible to
mpute exactly, it is generally agreed that when the ad-
rsaries are evenly matched (both technically and emo-
nally), the game is all dice. Over the short term, an aver-
e or good player can beat a superior player, but in the
ng run even the "unlucky" expert will win, for the law of
erages is as infallible as the law of gravity. We believe
at the proportion of luck to skill in backgammon is ap-

proximately 80 to 20, but a 20 percent edge is an ins
mountable advantage.

Take Las Vegas. If you play craps against the hou
and play correctly (that is, giving yourself the best chanc
the percentage in favor of the house is actually less thar
percent. But given that minuscule advantage, in the lo
run the house will win. In comparison, the 20 percent s
factor in backgammon is overwhelming.

As another example, what possibilities exist for hor
players when the track takes 15 to 17 percent out of ev
dollar they bet? None. You can only win consistently
the track if you have somehow fixed the race or have m
aged to obtain inside information. In backgammon,
understanding of the correct percentage moves in spec
situations qualifies as "inside information" and will
able you to win in the long run. But not every time, al
and often not even in what you believe to be crucial gam
This condition must be accepted philosophically,
course, and should not deter you from continuing a
tailed study of the game.

Backgammon is not a game in which luck should
taken seriously, though many players continue to gam
at it, apparently relying on the spurious advice of the
iental sage who claimed that if you threw a lucky man i
the sea, he would emerge with a fish in his mouth. Su
players forget that though *they* are gambling, the expe
are not. Gamesmen rather than gamblers, the experts
ways have an edge because they know infinitely m
about the game. Like many other endeavors, backgamm
is a game of levels; to play against the experts for money
nothing more than another version of Russian roulette.

Backgammon might be compared to *Alice in Wond
land*. On one level, that book can be described as a dr
fairy tale, but among the childish games, improbable ch
acters and laughter there is a subtle allegory that tells

ogether separate tale. In much the same way, backgam-
on can be learned and played forever as a rather simple
me of chance: once it is taken seriously, however, cun-
ng labyrinths and curious paradoxes begin to appear.
his book has attemped both to teach the beginner how to
ay and to enjoy the game, and to present at least a few of
e game's more intricate conundrums.

A note about kibitzing: If you are not directly involved
d are watching a match, no matter what happens at the
ole—repeat, no matter what—say nothing. Form any
inion you wish about the play or players, but remain si-
nt. Should some flagrant error astonish you, steal quietly
ay. When the match is over, but not until then, you can
proach either contestant and raise your questions or
jections, but never during play.

If an argument arises between the two players and you
el sure you know who is in the right and can show why,
ll say nothing—unless, and this is vital, you are ap-
aled to by *both* opponents.

Over the years, at tournaments and in money games,
e have seen specific positions presented to experts who
ll then argue the relative merits of the "right" move.
arely do they agree. At the end of these discussions, each
an will go his separate way convinced, however secretly,
at he was right and the rest of them were wrong. Back-
mmon seems not only to attract but to elicit the most
trageously egotistical behavior. If, for instance, a con-
ential questionnaire were sent to thirty acknowledged
perts and each was asked to fill in his choice for the one
st player in the world, you would get thirty different
minations, all autobiographical. More often than not,
e expert was not sure that he was right, but being an
xpert," he was expected to take a stand, which he will
hold for illogical reasons.

In bridge, for example, upon analysis the correct per-

centage play can almost always be determined, but thou
there are positions in backgammon where the proper mc
is self-evident, there are countless others where it is almc
impossible to get a majority opinion. In Diagram 93,
example, red has rolled a 6-4. What is the correct mov
There are at least three good options, but expert opini
is invariably divided.*

Which is as it should be. The game has few absolut
It is fluid and ever-changing, and often the best that o
can hope for is to sensibly exercise specific options. It i
game of calculated choices, which may be as humdrum

---

*First, you could cover your 2 point with the 4 and play the 6 in to your 5 po
White cannot escape on his next roll unless he rolls a 6-5, and even then h
vulnerable to a return 6-1. The reason for this choice is not that it is cons
ative but that it *forces* white to move. Any double is awkward, and shc
white not roll a 5 or a 6 he will (except for 2-1) have to put builders ou
play or weaken his five-point prime.

Secondly, you could hit white's blot on your 3 point, using a man fr
white's 12 point. This play leaves two blots in your board. It is true that wl
also has two blots, but these do not concern him much because he has a f
point prime, and every man of yours that is hit will have to get first to h
point and only then follow with a 6 to be free. If you choose to hit in an ef
to keep the lone white piece from escaping, you could be defeating your c
purpose because he may be prevented from moving at all, which could be
his advantage.

The third choice would be to hit his blot with the 4 from your bar pc
and to come out to his 10 point with the 6. This is wild, wide-open and in
inative, but it makes the next roll crucial. White could annihilate you
could be destroyed himself, depending on the dice. There is style and be
ness in this play, and if circumstances and the score are such that winni
gammon happens to be more advantageous to you than losing one is di
trous, you should consider taking this plunge.

Which of the three should you pick? An unequivocal answer is impo
ble. But this very fact is why backgammon is such a fascinating game.
course it is frustrating not to know for certain what to do. You *know* that
should make your 5 point with an opening 3-1, but as you progress you m
learn to improvise to the best of your ability, and the longer you play,
more aware you will become that a countless number of inscrutable dilem
like this example will occur.

Size up your opponent, the situation (is this a tournament or for mor
head-to-head or chouette?), and the score. Try to weigh every angle and t
choose what is best, considering the circumstances. We are not hedging wl
we say that a sound argument could be made for each of the three moves abc
depending on the situation.

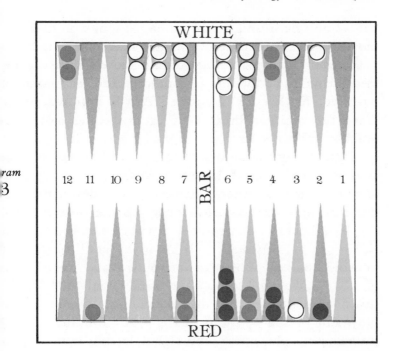

ram
3

centric as one wishes, but need not necessarily be "corct."

There is also a certain amount of gamesmanship to
employed in backgammon. As in any other competition,
is never advisable to appear nervous or uncomfortable
hen you sit down to play. This is particularly true when
u are opposed by a well-known player. Never greet him
saying, "You're too good for me. I'm only a beginner
d don't have a chance against someone like you." There
only one instance when you can say this: when you
n't mean a word of it! Given the uncertainties of the
me, you always have a chance, and with determination
d the dice you can upset the most expert of players.

If you tend to play slowly—and at first you probably

will—don't be intimidated by an opponent who rushes ŀ
moves. Take your time, no matter how much he hurri
you. Attempt to play your routine moves with a certa
steady rhythm and without hesitating needlessly—but or
when you feel secure in doing so. As you improve, you w
grasp the problem created by each specific move mo
quickly, and so make your plays with assurance and fina
ty. Occasionally, of course, there will be a difficult de‹
sion with which you'll have to take some time, and this
to be expected; in general, however, try to develop the ha
it of making your mind up fast and react accordingly.

The board is comparatively small, and your positi‹
and your opponent's are in front of you at all times, so
to avoid "balks." When part of your roll is "forced"—tŀ
is, if you have a 5-4 to play and there is only one 5—mo
this 5 immediately, and then concentrate on the best ‹
ployment of the 4. Many players will roll the dice a
immediately play the number, but having done so, th
will retract the move and make another play elsewhe
then vacillate again and make yet another move. Soon tŀ
are back to where they began and in a quandary. Sometim
it's difficult to choose the best percentage move, but try
train yourself to avoid this kind of play by thinking the s
uation through before touching your men. What it bo
down to is simply mental discipline, which is as valuab
in life as it is in a game. This sort of intangible is a val
able asset every time you sit down to play.

Size up your opponent immediately. Attempt to es
mate his strengths and weaknesses. If he is more expe
enced than you, use every legal ploy you have to equali
his edge. For instance, you should attempt to make eve
game as simple as possible. Against better players, alwa
seek simple positions. Block and run as best you ca
and at all times avoid back games. Further, if your opp

nt attempts to needle you, remain impervious. If he
lls, allow him to do so without becoming irritated. If he
ks, try not to listen, nor to fall into conversation. Con-
ntrate on the game at hand and ignore anything that
tervenes. Check all of your opponent's moves and remem-
r that it is not considered unethical to allow him to
ace his man in the wrong spot if it is to your advantage.

short, display as little emotion as possible, and try to
sregard bad luck or the fortune which may seem to favor
e enemy. The good player is one who does not com-
und his losses with personal feelings. "And yet," as one
pert has said, "99 percent of the people who play double
) when they are losing and draw back when they are
ead. You must look at backgammon in the same way
at you would look at a business reversal over which you
d no control." Of course this is a question of disci-
ine — but discipline is a quality that can be learned.

There is an interesting and complex psychological
ctor at work in the taking or dropping of a double. As-
me that in a chouette over a period of a few months cer-
in players dropped 1,000 games in which they were dou-
ed, and were correct 700 times and wrong 300, none of
hich was a gammon.

For many people the actual money gambled is not the
imary incentive. They enjoy the challenge and want to
in more for winning's sake than for receiving financial
wards. Such people like to be proved correct; it is part of
eir pleasure and boosts their egos. If you were able to
ok into these players' minds and psyches, you might find
at they actually *preferred* to be correct in their decisions
) percent of the time, even though they are subconscious-
aware that if they had been *wrong* 70 percent of the time
at is, if they had accepted all the doubles), they would be
tter off financially. The droppers of those thousand

games are minus 1,000 units; if they had taken, they wou
be minus 1,400 + 600, for a net of minus 800.

Many takable doubles are dropped because of such
outlook. Perhaps in these cases the individual is receivi
emotional fulfillment amply compensating him for l
lower financial rewards. We are not arguing for or agair
such eccentric behavior; we merely state that it exists a
occurs in many more instances than is realized.

As mentioned earlier, the ego is rampant throughc
the backgammon world (probably more unjustifiably th
in any other game, since the dice are the controlling fi
tor), and the desire to be "right" is neither consciou
recognized nor admitted by most players. It is a fac
worth thinking about, though, and perhaps there is a late
streak of it in all those people who drop too soon. T
point is, those players who drop takable doubles are pa
ing out good money that they don't have to lose.

When you do lose – and you will – try hard not to s
that your opponent out-lucked you. Nobody particula
cares that you missed two triple shots and that your opp
nent hit a 17 – 1 shot to win the whole match. But if t
provocation *is* too much and you must moan a little, *nev*
tell your opponent that he played a move incorrectly. Ev
if it is true, what have you gained? Restrain yourself, cc
gratulate him and contrive to smile! This is importa
because regardless of how good you are, you're going
gain considerable experience in being a loser.

Conversely, when you win, attempt to be gracious;
you have been lucky, admit it. No matter how badly yc
opponent behaves, neither argue nor disagree; after ;
you can afford to be generous.

The discipline that pervades the game should al
control the amount of money for which you play. This m
seem too obvious to dwell on, but more than a few play

volve themselves in high-stake games which invariably
eet with the predictable conclusion. If the amount of
oney you are playing for makes you uncomfortable, you
ould not be playing for that stake. That is the key to
hat you should play for. What you can "afford" is not
cessarily the stake at which you feel comfortable, wheth-
it is high or low. The two can be quite different. As-
me that you are a millionaire many times over. You can
fford" to play for almost any stake, but the chances are
at you would be uncomfortable long before you reached
e sum you could not afford. The amount to play for is
at which does not divert your attention from your main
ncern — the game.

This is not a lecture on how to conduct a life style or
attempt to dictate the stakes you should play for. Our
le purpose is to help you play in the most comfortable
ame of mind. Whether or not you have a fortune, if the
ake distresses you, simply decline to play in that particu-
r game. If you allow your ego to get the upper hand and
e seduced into a bigger game, you are at a distinct disad-
antage. You may out-luck it and win, but in the long run
u are a favorite to lose because you will inevitably drop
ubles that you should take, or not double when you
ould, for fear of increasing the stakes. Why expose your-
lf through false pride to such a situation?

To sum up: the stake that permits you to play at your
st is the stake that permits you to relax — regardless of
hat you can afford.

What we have been primarily concerned with in this
apter are the psychological traps into which every player
s periodically fallen. It is to these specific traps that we
ish to direct your attention, since if they are not recog-
ized and remedied, your backgammon talents will not
ogress beyond mere technical expertise. An eminent

neuropsychiatrist and analyst believes that to win at a[
game, you must first understand the specific skills i[
volved, and secondly the specific traps—that is, t[
psychology of the snares laid by your adversary. If y[
have mastered neither the skills nor the trap's alternativ[
and still insist on entering the game, you are throwing[
razor-sharp boomerang which will ultimately cut off yo[
own head. The psychiatrist goes on to say that the profe[
sionals of any game are those who place their opponents[
various categories, and then apply the trap most likely[
seduce them. It is the failure to recognize these traps a[
the subsequent inability to exert some rational control ov[
the course of events that not only indicate but instiga[
disaster.

This is yet another of the game's paradoxes, and pe[
haps its most important one. It is a game of war, a series[
all-or-nothing skirmishes conducted for the most part[
civilized company toward civilized ends. It is what Ni[
the Greek, that most infamous of American gamblers, ha[
in mind when, in discussing expert game-playing, he sai[
"It is the art of polite bushwhacking." Given the scope[
backgammon and its infinite possibilities, it is the co[
summate encounter.

◄12►

THREE GREAT GAMES

The common denominator of war
is the duel.
—*Karl von Clausewitz*

The following game took
ace between two of the best players in the country, and
llustrates much of what has been stressed throughout the
ook—for example, the vital importance of both 5 points.
o obtain these, inordinate risks should sometimes be tak-
n, and when both of them were secured, these two fine
ayers held them tenaciously, no matter how tempting the
nducements that were offered in an effort to break them.

Note also these players' ability to improvise, and to
djust their thinking to the constant flux in their respec-
ve positions. Risks are taken here, safe plays made there,
nd always the percentages are weighed.

In addition, the tremendous value of "owning" the
ube is graphically displayed in this game. This all-impor-
nt part of backgammon cannot be overemphasized. It has
een stressed again and again in the chapter on doubling,
nd here, in the end game below, is a practical demonstra-
on of what we have been trying to point out.

This specific game, played for high stakes, drew an
udience, and though the two opponents happened to be
iends, the ego factor began to emerge, as it usually does

when a crowd gathers, so both players gave it their be~~s~~
The result is backgammon of the highest caliber, full
imagination and expertise on both sides, and the read~~e~~
cannot help but learn from it if he plays it out, move f~~or~~
move, on his own board.

1. **Red** opens with a **6-1** and makes his bar.

1. **White** rolls a **4-1,** moving one man from red's 1
point to his own 9 point, and starting his own 5 point.

2. **R—5-1:** moves the 5 from white's 12 point to h~~is~~
own 8 point and drops the 1 from his 6 point to his 5 poir~~t~~
Both players are correctly trying to make their respecti~~ve~~
5 points.

2. **W—6-6:** makes his own bar with two men fro~~m~~
red's 12 point and establishes his own 2 point with tw~~o~~
men from his 8 point. This roll is too much too soon, b~~ut~~
what else can he do? It would be wrong to break the 1
point here.

3. **R—5-4:** hits white on his 5 point with man fro~~m~~
his 1 point and keeps going out to white's 10 point. ~~He~~
would prefer to make his own 5 point, but since he can~~'t~~
he is at least preventing his opponent from making hi~~s~~

3. **W—4-2:** enters on the 2 point and hits red's m~~an~~
on the 5 point with man from red's 1 point.

4. **R—5-4:** here red could enter on either the 4 or t~~he~~
5 point and continue on to hit white on the 9 point, b~~ut~~
instead chooses the correct tactic of entering on the 5 a~~nd~~
then making this point with the man from the 1 point.

4. **W—4-2:** white in turn makes his opponent's
point with man from red's 1 point and starts his own
point with man from his 6 point. He is leaving two blo~~ts~~
in his outer board because he is trying to lure red off h~~is~~
own 5 point. Once again, an example of correct expe~~rt~~
tactics which are seldom, if ever, followed in average co~~m~~
petition. (See Diagram 94.)

5. **R—2-1:** starts his own 4 point with man from his
point and moves man from white's 10 point to white's 11
point, leaving 2's everywhere. At this moment red doesn't
mind being hit, and this play gives him diversification.

5. **W—4-3:** moves the blot from his 8 point and covers his own 4 point, and starts his 3 point by moving off
his 6 point. He is still leaving the blot on his 9 point to
try to tempt red to break the vital 5 point.

6. **R—4-3:** red correctly refuses the bait. With man
from 8 point he covers the blot on his 4 point, and plays
the blot on white's 11 point to his own 11 point. With this
he is vulnerable to a 6, but to his opponent's cost of breaking the 5 point. (Alternatively, this roll could have been
played from white's 11 and 12 points to red's 10 point, thus

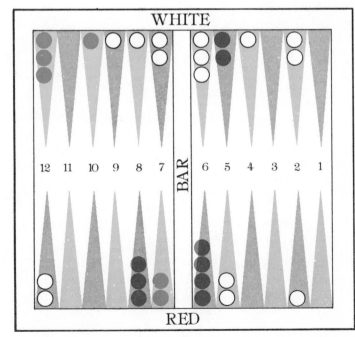

Diagram
4

WHITE

12 11 10 9 8 7 BAR 6 5 4 3 2 1

RED

blocking white's 5's. This move also has merit, and sor
experts might prefer it.)

6. **W—5-3**: with the 3 he moves from red's 2 point
the 5 point, and finally saves the man on his 9 point
moving it in to the 4 point. To come out all the way wi
the back man would leave red with too many options.

7. **R—5-3**: moves the blot on his 11 point all the w
to start his 3 point.

7. **W—5-4**: moves one man from red's 5 point all t
way to his own 11 point, making him vulnerable to a
But at what cost to red!

8. **R—5-2**: moves both men in from his 8 point, cove
ing his 3 point and improving his board. Since white
clinging tenaciously to his 5 point, red's 8 point has litt
value at this stage.

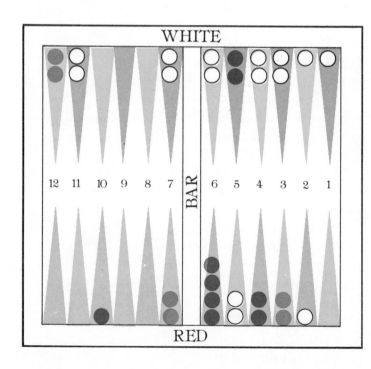

Dia
9

8. **W—2-1:** There are some interesting choices here. hite's is to cover the 3 point in his board with the 1 and play the 2 from red's 12 point to his own 11 point to ock red's 6's. By doing so he gives three extra shots (4-5-3, 3-5) at the blot on red's 12 point, but considers at blocking red's 6's is worth it. He could also have oved all the way from the 11 point to the 8 point, leaving ly a 3, but in our opinion his move was much superior.

9. **R—2-1:** hits white's blot on the 12 point with man om white's 12 point and continues on to his own 10 int. A questionable play. It might have been better if red d split off his own 6 point; there's no need to take any sks at this particular stage of the game. This is perhaps e only error by either player in the game, and it is a mi-or one. Still, unless white gets the "miracle roll" of dou-e 5's, it is doubtful that he would break his anchor to hit d were his next roll, say, 5-1 or 5-2.

9. **W—2-1:** enters on the 2 and plays the 1 from his vn 2 point to his 1 point. Playing the 1 in this way is rtually forced, but these two open blots in white's home ard will strongly affect the strategy of both players nceforth. Indeed, red promptly doubles because of these o open men in white's board, and because white's tim-g is bad. White accepts. (See Diagram 95.)

10. **R—4-2:** brings the blot in from his own 10 point l the way. He doesn't hit white on his 2 point because if hite does not roll a 6 or a 3, he may have to play a man men elsewhere in the board he does not want to move.

10. **W—4-4:** moves two men out to red's 9 point, at st breaking the 5 point, and two men from his 11 point his bar. An awkward shot, but at least he has men to ay now.

11. **R—4-3:** hits white's blot on his 2 point with man om his 6 point, and moves out to white's 8 point with e 3, leaving 2's everywhere. A roll of 2-2 by white now

would be a disaster, but the risk is worthwhile. To mo
the 3 from his own 6 point to his 3 point would of cou
be safer, but it is awkward and craven.

11. **W—5-3:** enters on the 5 point and continues c
to the 8 point. A good shot for white; if he had been forc
to hit red's blot on the 2 point and not been able to co
those in his board, it could have been the beginning
the end.

12. **R—4-1:** hits white's blot on the 8 point with
man from white's 12 point. Red is going all out offensive
now because of white's two blots, and is correct in his c
cision not to make his own 2 point.

12. **W—6-5:** enters on the 5 point, and with the 6
at last able to cover one of the blots in his board. (See D
gram 96.)

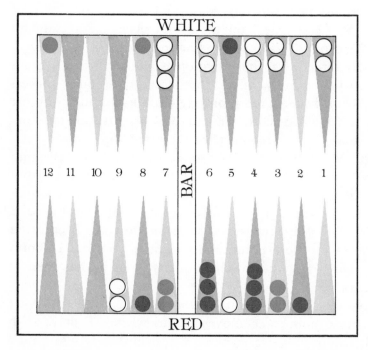

Di

13. **R — 5-3:** There are several choices here. For in-
nce, red could cover his 2 point from his bar point and
white's blot on the 5 point, but this would leave five
ts open around the board, and if he were hit and could
come in, even for a single roll, he might lose a gam-
n. Instead he rightly chooses to play conservatively,
ering his 8 point with the 5 and making white's 8 point
h the 3.

13. **W — 5-4:** moves out to red's 9 point with the 4,
covers his own 2 point with the 5, establishing a five-
nt board.

14. **R — 4-1:** covers his 2 point with man from his bar,
ablishing a four-point board.

14. **W — 3-2:** brings one man in all the way from the
, leaving one man out so that he won't be forced to play
ossibly awkward 6 from red's 9 point.

15. **R — 6-5:** makes his own 1 point with men from his
nd 7 points. He could run with one of his back men, but
s is risky — particularly because there is no assurance
t he will be able to get by next time, and may have to
ve an 8 again.

15. **W — 5-4:** moves all the way from red's 9 point to
own bar point.

16. **R — 5-2:** moves one of the men on his 8 point all
way in to the 1 point. He too is leaving a man out, just
white did earlier, in case he has an awkward 6 to play.

16. **W — 5-2:** this time white plays both men in off his
, figuring that red on his next move will have to either
ak his board or move off white's 8 point. White wants
keep his board intact in case he gets this indirect shot.

17. **R — 4-4:** moves the two men from white's 8 point
he 12 point, and two men off the 6 point to the 2 point,
leaving himself a playable 6. (See Diagram 97.)

17. **W — 6-3:** a very interesting decision for white:

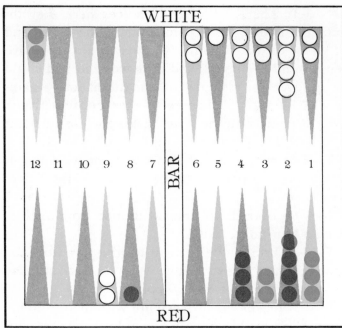

should he leave a 1 shot or a 4 shot? If he leaves a 4 and
not hit, red is slowed up drastically unless he gets b
men on white's 12 point past white with a very good re
Yet to leave a 4 shot instead of a 1 is giving red 4 ex
chances (15 instead of 11). After much reflection, wh
decides that red's position in a potential race is too stro
so he leaves the 4 shot and plays one man all the way
his bar.

18. **R—5-2:** white's play pays off. Red has to play
man from his 8 point down to his 1 point.

18. **W—3-2:** moves his back man safely to his own
point.

19. **R—5-1:** moves both men off white's 12 point
red's 12 and 8 points.

19. **W—5-1:** moves both outside men onto the 6 point.

20. **R—5-2:** moves the man on the 12 point all the
y in to the 5 point.

20. **W—4-1:** takes a man off his 4 point and his 1
nt.

21. **R—4-2:** moves his last man in from the 8 point to
4 point and takes a 2 off.

21. **W—4-3:** takes two men off.

22. **R—6-1:** takes two men off.

22. **W—3-2:** takes two men off.

23. **R—6-2:** takes two men off.

23. **W—6-2:** takes two off.

24. **R—4-1:** takes two off.

24. **W—5-2:** takes two off.

25. **R—6-5:** takes two off.

25. **W—2-1:** takes two off.

Up till now, both players have rolled fairly well in
ring off, considering that there have been no doubles,
t though red has been slightly in the lead all the way,
advantage hasn't been really clear-cut until now. But
ite owns the doubler and red can do nothing but roll
d hope. The advantage of having the cube on your side
graphically illustrated here. If it was red's turn to double
d he did so now, white would be hard put to accept, but
ce white has the doubler, he is in this game till the very
d and cannot be forced out.

Look at Diagram 98 and note that there is yet one
•re fascinating paradox here. With three men on the 6
int, 3-3 would be a better roll for white than 4-4, even
•ugh the latter roll has 4 more total pips! This is one
•re example of the distortions of the pip count.

26. **R—5-4:** takes two men off.

26. **W—5-1:** takes one man off his 6 point.

27. **R—3-1:** takes two men off.

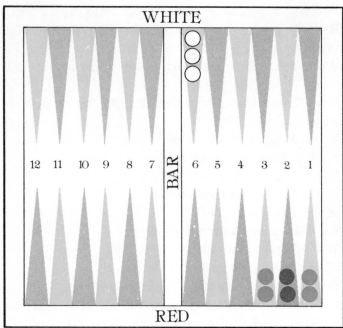

Dia
Q

27. **W—4-4:** wins the game on his last shot with ▌
only double. Only 6-6, 5-5, 4-4 or 3-3 win for white in t▌
position, making him an 8 to 1 underdog, but as is so oft▌
the case, because he had the cube he was able to hang in▌
the end and pull the game out at the last possible instant▌

◀▶

A few years ago during a pause in a major tournam▌
in the Caribbean, two of the top entrants challenged ea▌
other to a few head-to-head money games. After all, w▌
else could they do for relaxation? One of their games v▌
the following, and it is worth close study.

1. **R – 5-2:** moves two men over from white's 12 point.

1. **W – 3-3:** makes his own 5 point and moves two men to his opponent's 4 point to thwart red's builder on the point.

2. **R – 3-3:** also makes his 5 point and moves up in his ponent's board to the 4 point. An alternative would be to ck white's 6's by moving two men to red's 10 point, but play is better.

2. **W – 4-3:** hits red's blot on the 11 point with man m red's 4 point. A good play, because red can now only white with 4's and 2's anywhere in the board.

3. **R – 4-3:** enters on the 3 point and hits white's blot his own 4 point with man from his 8 point. He should t even consider for an instant breaking his anchor on ite's 4 point and hitting white's blot on the 8 point.

3. **W – 2-1:** enters on the 1 point and saves his blot on : 8 point by moving it in to his 6 point. White must re-nch at this moment because he has no defense.

4. **R – 3-3:** There are lots of choices here. Red choos-to make the 3 point in his own board with two men from . 6 point, to hit white's blot with his own blot on the 1 int, and to bring a man down from white's 12 point to own 10 point. This is a great shot, for if white fails to er, it will be extremely hard for him to accept a double light of his open man on red's 11 point.

4. **W – 4-3:** enters on the 4 point and hits red's blot on ite's 3 point with man from his 6 point. It is mandatory white to hit here in order to try to keep red busy, there-protecting his open man on red's 4 point.

5. **R – 6-2:** enters on white's 2 point and hits white's t on his own 4 point with the 6. Note that had white not red in his previous roll, the 6-2 would have pointed on ite here.

5. **W – 6-3:** cannot enter.

At this point red gives a good gambling double. I has gammon possibilities, and white's position is perilo. But white daringly takes in this position; he is perha showing off a bit because of the audience. (See Diagra 99.)

6. **R — 6-5:** red covers his 1 point with man from his point and starts his bar with man from white's 12 poi. He is going all out to blitz white if he doesn't enter on h next roll.

6. **W — 6-4:** a saving shot for white. He enters on the point, hitting red's blot, and continues on out to the point.

7. **R — 6-2:** enters on white's 2 point and starts his ov

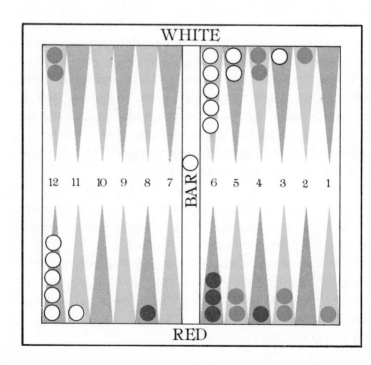

Dia

ς

point with man from his 8 point. He does not save the
▸en man on white's 12 point because suddenly he needs
▸dly to delay; having made his own 1 point, he is far too
▸vanced at this stage of the game.

7. **W—3-2:** covers the 3 point in his own board with
▸an from his 6 point and hits red on the 12 point with the
This is a close decision, but red's board is now just good
▸ough so that white feels he should avoid giving a direct
▸ot.

8. **R—5-2:** enters on the 2 point and continues on out
▸ the bar. Again, he does not make his own 2 point be-
▸use he is ahead of himself.

8. **W—5-5:** hits red on the bar with man from his 12
▸int and makes his 8 point with three men from red's 12
▸int. He does not make his 1 point because he wants red
▸ come in and be forced to play.

9. **R—6-2:** has to enter on the 2, and to avoid breaking
▸s forward anchor must play the 6 from his 7 point to his
▸point. Red is now in a very bad position. (See Diagram
▸0.)

White now correctly redoubles. It is a bad emotional
▸ke by red—but he takes nonetheless, as happens with
▸en the best of players from time to time.

9. **W—4-4:** a great roll. Makes his bar with the man
▸ red's 10 point, and makes the 9 point with the two men
▸ red's 12 point, establishing a five-point prime.

10. **R—4-1:** moves two men off his 6 point, making
▸e 2 point. This could have been worse; he still has a
▸ur-point board.

10. **W—6-4:** moves both men in off the 9 point.

11. **R—5-2:** a tremendous saving shot for red, giving
▸m a chance. Needless to say, he moves the back man off
▸e 2 point all the way out.

11. **W—6-4:** brings both men in off the bar.

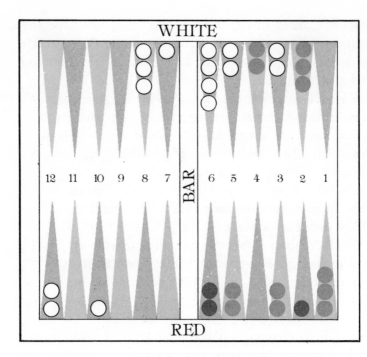

Diag
1C

12. **R—3-2:** moves from white's 9 point to his own
point.

12. **W—5-4:** moves his forced 4 from his 5 point in
his 1 point, and the 5 from his 6 point also to the 1 poin
By moving the 5 this way rather than bringing it in fro
outside, white still has two builders to bear if red decid
to break his forward anchor.

13. **R—6-1:** starts his 4 point by moving all the w
from his 11 point.

13. **W—5-1:** moves the 5 from the 8 point in to the
point, and the 1 from the 6 point to the 5 point.

14. **R—4-3:** moves a man from the 4 point out
white's 11 point. Red feels that he can't afford to spoil h
board any further and must break his forward anchor.

14. **W—6-2:** has no 6, so moves the 2 to the 1 point.

15. **R—4-1:** makes the 4 point with the 1, securing a
e-point board, and moves the 4 from white's 11 point to
; own 10 point. (See Diagram 101.)

15. **W—5-1:** There are a wealth of fascinating critical
cisions to be made with this roll. White could hit on the
point and move a man in from the 8 point. But this
uld leave two men open, which is dangerous, consider-
g red's five-point board. Secondly, he could play both
tside men, saving one and leaving only one man open to
3 or a 5. But white chooses to play conservatively and
fely, taking both men off his 6 point.

16. **R—4-2:** a good shot. Red starts both 6 points.

16. **W—6-6:** cannot play.

17. **R—2-1:** again a tough choice. Red finally decides

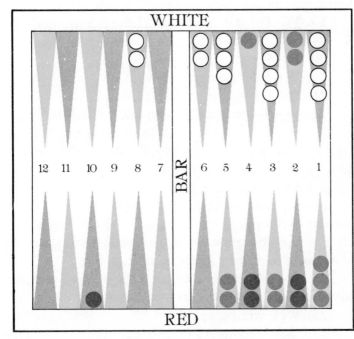

ram
)1

to come out all the way to white's 9 point, relying on h
back anchor to get a shot later.

17. **W—2-1:** another intriguing decision. The be
immediate percentage for white is to give red a 2 shot I
starting the 4 point, but on his next roll he might not I
able to cover, and might even have to leave two men ope
In these circumstances white decides to move one outsi
man to his 5 point and gamble against a 6—a 20 to 16 sh
in his favor because 3-3 doesn't hit.

18. **R—1-1:** moves from white's 9 point to red's
point.

18. **W—4-2:** moves the outside man in to the 4 poi
with the 4, and moves a man from his 5 point to his
point, leaving four men on his 5 point. If he left five me
there, a 6-6 or 5-5 on the next roll would leave two blots.

19. **R—6-4:** covers the 6 point, giving him a close
board, and moves the 4 to white's 6 point.

19. **W—6-3:** takes a man off the 5 point and saves t
blot by moving it to the 1 point.

20. **R—5-3:** moves from W6 to R11.

20. **W—5-1:** takes two men off.

21. **R—1-1:** moves from R11 to R7.

21. **W—3-1:** takes two men off.

22. **R—5-1:** moves from the bar to the 1 point, pi
ning all his hopes on getting a shot on the next roll, f
with his next 6 he will be forced to leave.

22. **W—4-1:** has options, but must leave a blot. Ta
ing another man off is desirable, but not at the cost of gi
ing red two extra shots (2-1, 1-2) if he leaves the blot c
his 5 point; therefore he moves both men down, the 4
the 1 point and the 1 to the 4 point.

23. **R—3-2:** hits the blot on the 4 point and moves c
out to white's bar.

23. **W:** cannot play.

Red now redoubles in this position. He is a favori

ere because white has only five men off. But because of
ne men on red's 1 point, white accepts the double, for the
nances are that red is going to have to break his board
nmediately without getting any of the extra men off *before* he has to break. White's take is correct in all money
ames. (See Diagram 102.)

24. **R—3-1:** from W7 to W11.

24. **W:** cannot play.

25. **R—2-1:** from W11 to R11.

25. **W:** cannot play.

26. **R—6-4:** moves his outside man all the way to the
point, justifying white's take even more.

26. **W:** cannot play.

27. **R—4-1:** bears one man off the 4 point and moves
ne other man down to the 3 point. Red doesn't leave a blot

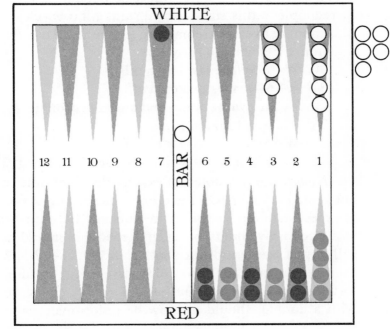

gram
02

because he has a chance to win even if white rolls the
immediately — though of course 4-4 would probably be di
astrous.

27. **W — 2-2:** cannot enter.

28. **R — 2-2:** takes two men off his 2 point, and move
two men down from his 6 to his 4 point.

28. **W — 4-1:** cannot enter.

29. **R — 5-4:** bears one man off his 5 point and save
the other by moving it to his 1 point.

29. **W — 5-5:** enters on the 5 point and goes all the wa
to his own 5 point. This "miracle" roll puts white rigl
back in the game.

30. **R — 6-1:** takes two men off.

Should white redouble now? Though he has only fi
men off to red's six, it is his roll, and if he can continue t
take two men off on each subsequent roll, he will win th
game, barring doubles. But under no circumstances shoul
he redouble at this stage. Any 2 ruins him; besides, with
minimum of five rolls remaining (if neither player throws
double), it is much too early.

30. **W — 6-5:** takes two men off.

31. **R — 6-4:** takes two men off.

Once again white waits and doesn't redouble, for the
any 2 would lose him the game.

31. **W — 5-1:** takes two men off.

32. **R — 6-3:** takes two men off. (See Diagram 103.)

Now white redoubles, at exactly the right time; he ha
not waited too long. On the other hand, red must take; an
2 except double 2's will win outright for him becaus
white certainly could not accept a redouble should he no
roll any of the ten losing shots (2-1, 2-3, 2-4, 2-5, 2-6, c
their reciprocals). By redoubling here, white is admittedl
forfeiting two probable further rolls for a chance to wi
with a double, should he now be unfortunate enough t

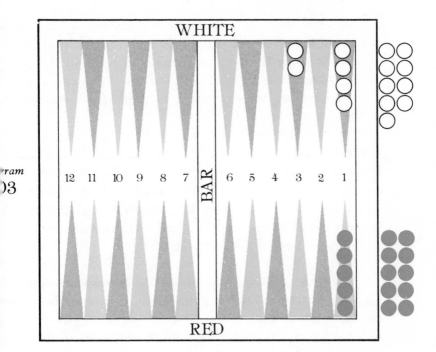

ram
)3

oll a single 2. (That is, if white did *not* double here and
hen proceeded to roll a 2, red could not redouble him,
nce he would not own the cube, and white would have
wo turns to win by rolling a double.) But this chance
hould be taken, and his double here is technically and
actically sound—as is red's acceptance of it. Many players
would drop if they were red in this position, but they are
bsolutely wrong. In this case, however, red correctly ac-
epts white's double.

32. **W—3-1:** takes two men off. Now (assuming no
oubles) only a 2-1 will lose for white.

33. **R—6-5:** takes two men off.

33. **W—5-4:** takes two men off.

Red now needs any double to win, and is a 5 to 1 un-

derdog. The doubler is at 16, and the stake is $5 a poin
How much should red offer, and how much should whi
accept, to settle their game here? You have all the equi
ment to work this out, so why not see if you can come u
with the answer before reading further? (If necessary, ref
to the chapter on settlements.)

In this particular situation, red offers to give $50, an
white counters by stating that he will take $60. These o
fers show that both men know what they are doing, be
cause $50 is too low and $60 is too high. They haggle for
while, and finally settle on $55, which is about right. Th
nearest figure is between $53 and $54, so white receives
little bit the best of the settlement.

Even though both opponents in this game were fir
players, it shows how the emotions can sometimes tak
over and affect anyone's reason. In particular we feel tha
red was wrong in accepting white's redouble on the nint
move—despite the fact that in this book we advocate th
philosophy of taking a double whenever there is a doub
But red's position at this stage was almost untenable, an
he should have dropped, as most good players would hav
Hence, in this particular game justice was done, becaus
after this foolhardy take, red did not deserve to win.

What follows is a game recently played by two of th
world's best in a tournament match in London that wa
televised and followed with great interest by player
around the world.

White opened the game with a roll of 6-1 and made hi
bar point. Red rolled a 6-4, running out from white's

int to white's 11 point. White rolled a 5-2, hitting red's
o blots on his 11 point and 1 point. Red then rolled a 5-
coming in twice and hitting white's blot on the 1 point.
hitting contest then ensued, with each player attempting
establish a position, being hit, and forced in turn to hit
ain. The moves are listed below.

3. **W — 5-6:** enters on red's 5-point and hits red's blot
own 5 point with man from 11 point.

3. **R — 2-1:** enters on white's 2 point and hits white's
ot on own 5 point with man from 6 point.

4. **W — 3-4:** enters on red's 3 point and hits red's blot
his 5 point with man from 1 point.

4. **R — 5-6:** enters, hitting white's blot on his 5 point,
d continues on to white's 11 point.

5. **W — 3-2:** enters on red's 3 point and hits on white's
point with man from red's 12 point.

5. **R — 2-1:** enters on white's 2 point and hits on own 5
int with man from 6 point.

6. **W — 4-2:** enters on red's 2 point and hits on red's 5
int with man from his 1 point.

6. **R — 3-1:** enters on white's 3 point and hits on own 5
int with man from 6 point.

This was the first really major decision in the game.
ee Diagram 104.) Red's option was to come in on the 1
int, establishing two blocks, and to hit with the 3 from
s 8 point. But the move as played is imaginative and dar-
g. If red had come in on the 1 point, he would have been
mmitting himself to a back game. Red can afford the
ay he made because white has made only his bar and has
t yet made any points in his inner board. Hence, red is
t necessarily in a back game as yet. The drawback to
is play, however, is that red has lost a builder by hitting
hite's blot from his 6 point instead of from the 8 point.
onetheless, this is an interesting example of early tactics.

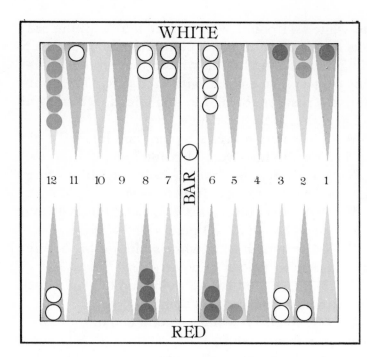

Red has decided against a back game this early in th
game—going along with the theory that back game
should if possible be avoided.

7. **W—3-1:** enters on red's 1 point and hits blot o
red's 5 point with man from 2 point.

7. **R—1-6:** enters on white's 1 point and starts his ow
bar point with man from white's 12 point.

8. **W—6-1:** makes own 5 point with men from 6 poir
and 11 point.

By far his best choice. He, of course, could have h
red's blot on the bar point, but this would serve no pu
pose, since white has too many of red's men in his inn
board already.

8. **R—3-1:** moves from white's 1 point to white's

int and makes his own bar point with man from his 8
int.

Another interesting play. (See Diagram 105.) Red
ght have left the blot on his bar point and made white's
oint instead. Another alternative would have been to hit
ite's blot on red's 5 point with the 3 and to make the 3
int in white's board with the 1. But both of these moves
uld commit him to a back game, which he is still reluc-
t to get involved in. But because white now has his 5
int and a four-point block, we believe that red should
ve made the move. However, we imagine that red,
eing that white had four men in his inner board, was still
empting to avoid a back game. In this case, we feel he
s wrong. White's four back men do give him good tim-

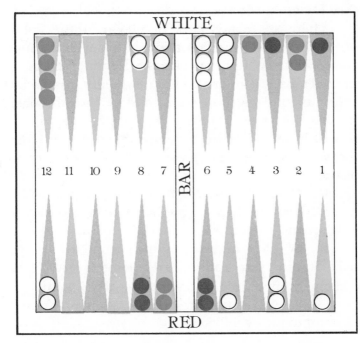

am
5

ing to defend a back game, however, and red decid
against it.

At this point, white doubles red to 2. It is interesti
to speculate on whether or not white would have doubl
if red had used the 1 to make white's 4 point. Despite t
fact that white has a good position, it is still a bold doub
Red has no serious flaws in his game. He has a defensi
anchor and opportunities for delay, and white is short
builders in his outer board. Red must have felt the sam
since he accepted white's double.

9. **W—5-3:** makes own 3 point with men from his
point and 8 point, hitting red.

9. **R—6-5:** cannot enter.

10. **W—3-3:** makes his own 4 point with two m
from his bar point and moves one from red's 12 point
white's 10 point and one from red's 1 point to red's 4 poi
(See Diagram 106.)

There are many ways of playing these double 3
With two of red's men on the bar already and a four-poi
board, white could have made the 1 point, thereby sabot
ing red's back game entirely. Admittedly it is an awkwa
and unnatural move to make, but well worth consideri
in this instance. But having rejected it, white sur
should have started his bar with the fourth 3, rather th
the weak and aimless move up to the 4 point in re
board.

10. **R—3-1:** enters on the 1 point. A great roll for r
he still has one man on the bar, but he has secured th
vital second point in his opponent's board.

11. **W—2-2:** moves two men from red's 3 point
red's 5 point, one from red's 12 point to white's 11 poi
and one from white's 10 point to white's 8 point.

11. **R—4-1:** enters on 1 point and moves from white
12 point to his own 9 point.

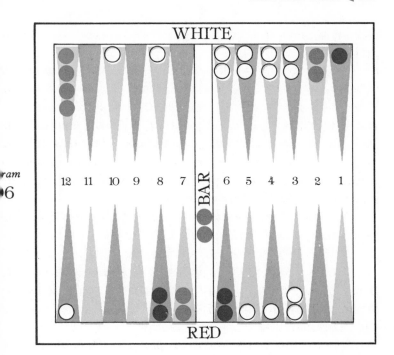

12. **W—5-2:** moves from red's 5 point to red's 12
int, not hitting red's blot with the man from red's 4
int. This is the correct play. White does not want to de-
y red further and so declines to hit. At this juncture, he
s a distinct edge in every area. He even holds his ene-
y's 5 point.

12. **R—3-1:** red hits white's blot on red's 12 point
th man from white's 12 point and moves the 3 from
ite's 12 point to his own 10 point. (See Diagram 107.)

This is one of the most fascinating decisions of the
me. If white's two men on the 5 point had been on the 4
int, we are sure that red would have blocked his 9 point
th the 3-1, thereby containing white's three men in his
ner board unless white rolled a 6. In this position white

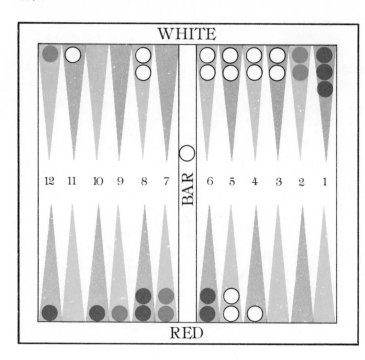

Dia
1(

has very little in reserve and might easily be forced in
breaking his blockade. But since the men were on the
point, red elected to go into a massive back game. An i
genious and daring play.

13. **W—4-3:** enters on 3 point and moves from red's
point to red's 9 point, hitting red's blot. White still do
not relish hitting, but in order to break up red's counterii
blockade, he decides to attack. If he had entered on the
point and played the 3 to his own 8 point, he could
blocked with low numbers. Double 3's would be especial
disastrous. A good example of going against the usual
sound premise of not hitting in a back game. The situati
is unique, and white correctly improvised.

13. **R—5-5:** unable to enter.

14. **W—2-1:** moves men on red's 3 and 4 points up to
s 5 point. White might have hit two more of red's men,
t rightly decided to bring two men up. An expert play.

14. **R—6-1:** enters on 1 point and springs to white's
r point.

15. **W—5-2:** moves from red's 5 point to red's 10
int, hitting, and from red's 9 point to red's 11 point.
ere again, white makes a crucial error, in our opinion.
ie 2 is vital. Following the practice of not hitting when
u are defending against a back game, white does not hit
ice—but he should have. It is a time to ensure that red
es not make white's bar point by rolling a 6-1, 6-2 or
2, a total of six shots. (He should not use 5-1 to hit, be-
use the 2 point is too valuable.) It is a calculated risk, but
: think white was in error here. If white secures his bar
d establishes a prime, he has an excellent chance to con-
in his opponent's men long enough so that red's remain-
g forces will be well out of play. In other words, red's
her men will have been forced to move to the forward
ints in his inner board before white's blockade breaks.

15. **R—5-2:** enters on the 2 point and makes white's
r point. Because white did not hit twice and red did roll
e 5-2, he has come from far behind and is about even
oney now. (See Diagram 108.)

16. **W—5-5:** moves two men from red's 5 point to
d's 10 point, one from red's 11 point to white's 9 point,
d one from white's 11 point to white's 6 point. A very
utious play. What is white afraid of? He wants to be hit,
d by playing safely he has made himself too fast.

16. **R—5-3:** moves his two men from his 8 point to his
point and 3 point, deliberately leaving two blots. It is
tirely to his advantage to be hit, and if white rolls 3's
d/or 2's, he will have to hit or strip his board. Curiously,
nce white does not want to hit under any circumstances,

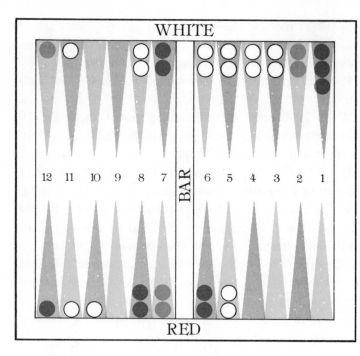

Diag
1O

red is partially "blocking" white with his two separate blots.

17. **W—6-2:** moves from red's 10 point to white's point, and from white's 6 point to white's 4 point. Aga white is dogging it by playing safe. Red has perfect timi now.

17. **R—6-3:** moves from white's 1 point to white's 1 point, leaving yet another blot.

18. **W—6-4:** moves from red's 10 point to white's point, and from red's 10 point to white's 11 point.

18. **R—4-1:** moves from red's 12 point to red's 8 poin and from red's 7 point to red's 6 point. There is no point i hitting; he has no board.

19. **W—5-1:** moves from white's 9 point to white's

int, and from white's 11 point to white's 6 point, refus-
g to hit, of course.

19. **R—2-2:** red's first usable double of the game; he
es it to make two good points in his board (i.e., one man
7 to R5, one man R8 to R4, and one man R6 to R4).

20. **W—6-1:** moves from white's 9 point to white's 8
int, and from white's 9 point to white's 3 point. A good
ot, but red's timing is still excellent.

20. **R—3-3:** covers the man on his 3 point (W10 to
3), giving him a four-point board.

21. **W—6-4:** moves from W8 to W4. He cannot play a

21. **R—5-4:** W7 to W11 and W12 to R8.
22. **W—3-1:** W8 to W5 and W4 to W3, not hitting. He

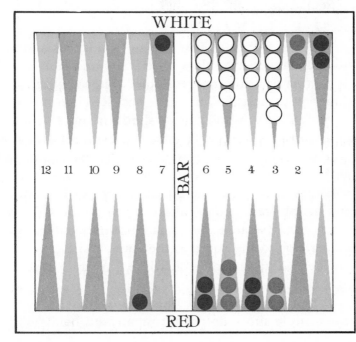

ram
9

does not want to delay red.

22. **R−5-4:** W11 to R5.

23. **W−5-3:** W8 to W5 and W8 to W3.

As can be seen in Diagram 109, white has no
brought all of his men into his inner board, but red's tir
ing remains nearly perfect.

23. **R−3-1:** R8 to R7 and W7 to W10.

24. **W−5-2:** bears one off the 5 point and moves fro
W6 to W4.

24. **R−4-1:** W10 to R10.

25. **W−1-1:** W6 to W5 twice and W5 to W3.

25. **R−6-2:** R10 to R2.

26. **W−5-1:** bears one off the 5 point and W4 to W
keeping his men as diversified as possible.

26. **R−5-1:** R7 to R2 and R5 to R4.

27. **W−4-2:** bears one off the 4 point and W5 to W3
a forced move.

27. **R−4-1:** W2 to W7.

28. **W−5-4:** bears two men off and leaves a triple sh
which endangers two blots. (See Diagram 110.)

In this position, red redoubled. Should white take? I
all money games, the answer is yes. Red can hit with ar
2, 3 or 4, which means that 27 shots hit and 9 do not, mal
ing him exactly a 3 to 1 favorite. You will recall that 3 to
is the dividing line on whether or not one accepts a dou
ble. In this instance, white is neither over nor under. Bu
the determining factor here is that if red misses, white ha
good double-game possibilities, since he has five men o
already. But because this was a tournament match, an
due perhaps to the score at the time or the psychologic;
blow he had just been dealt, white thought it expedient t
drop.

When a position like this arises — that is, when yo
leave a triple shot — do not throw up your hands in the be

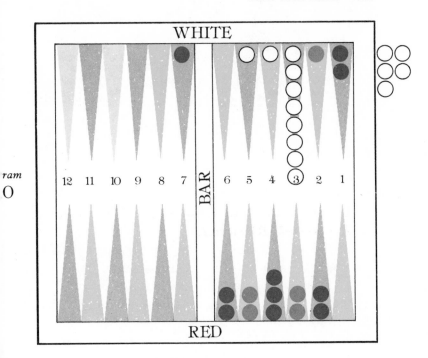

ram
0

f that your cause is hopeless. How many times, for ex-
mple, have you failed to enter a three-point board? In this
stance the odds are exactly the same. But red may have
uffed white here. The psychological setback of suddenly
aving two blots may have caused him to drop without
nsidering the position carefully.

Nevertheless, overall this is a superb game by two
eat strategists, and it demonstrates the essence of back-
mmon.

About the Authors

RCLAY COOKE was born in 1912, and graduated from Yale in 1934.
r a year thereafter he worked as a roustabout in the oil fields in the
uth, then for a bank in New York City, but when he found that this
interfered with his attendance at Yankee Stadium, the Polo
ounds and Ebbets Field, he left with no regrets.

Though Mr. Cooke is widely acknowledged to be one of the three
four best backgammon players extant, he feels that his true métier is
a big-league baseball manager, a post which will never be offered
m.

Mr. Cooke is married, has four children, and lives in Englewood,
w Jersey, and during the season can be found in the second row of
e Metropolitan Opera orchestra every Friday night.

N BRADSHAW was born in the United States in 1937 and has lived in
gland for most of his adult life. He is an amateur backgammon
ayer, a professional writer, and the author of *Fast Company,* a comi-
l study of the good works and bad habits of six American gamblers.